Gunni
For Glory

C000121551

Other Books by Simon & Schuster
in conjunction with the *Daily Express*

Champions: The 26 Year Quest for Glory
The Story of Manchester United's Winning Season 92-3

Double Winners
The Full Story of Manchester United's Victorious 93-4 Season

Nigel Mansell: World Champion

For news, reports and independent information on Arsenal in
the 1994/5 season call 0891-337-706. The service will be regularly
updated from 6 August 1994.

For the latest scores, news and classified results throughout the
1994/5 soccer season call the *Daily Express* Soccer Line 0891-118-888.

Calls cost 39p per minute cheap rate and 49p per minute at all other times.
Prices correct at going to press.

Gunning For Glory

The Full Story of Arsenal's Victorious 93-4 Season

Compiled by
DAVID EMERY

SIMON & SCHUSTER
LONDON · SYDNEY · NEW YORK · TOKYO · SINGAPORE · TORONTO

First published in Great Britain by Simon & Schuster Ltd, 1994
A Paramount Communications Company

Copyright © Express Newspapers plc, 1994

This book is copyright under the Berne Convention
No reproduction without permission
All rights reserved

Simon & Schuster Ltd
West Garden Place
Kendal Street
London W2 2AQ

Simon & Schuster of Australia Pty Ltd
Sydney

A CIP catalogue record for this book is available from the British
Library.

0-671-71368-X

Typesetting and origination by SLG Business Services

Printed in Great Britain by The Bath Press

Contents

Foreword

I don't think I have ever experienced such elation over a single goal. The one I scored against Liverpool when we beat them 2-0 on the final day of the season to win the title in 1989 must run it close.

But that strike in Copenhagen which brought the Cup Winners' Cup to Highbury will live with me for the rest of my life as my finest memory of football.

You can stand on the practice ground and attempt to hit a shot a hundred times, but you are never truly sure if you have mastered the technique until the chance comes in the heat of battle. I'd tried that left foot shot a thousand times over the years but I'd never hit a sweeter one than I did against Parma.

I can remember it all so wonderfully clearly. The ball dropped in between my feet but I managed to get a clean sweep at it with my left foot and it sped in off a post. If you can choose where to put the ball, that is the perfect spot.

My overwhelming feeling was sheer delight that I had been able to repay the fans for so much of their support and loyalty to me over the seven years I have spent at Highbury since leaving Leicester.

They have been great years and, even if the manager now decides he needs to buy a younger striker, I will always remember my time with Arsenal with great warmth and satisfaction. Together we have won two League titles, the League Cup, the FA Cup and now the Cup Winners' Cup. I feel I got in at the start of this great era; the only honour I missed was the first League Cup triumph over Liverpool.

The last two years have been disappointing to me. I have struggled to maintain a place with Kevin Campbell scrapping it out with me to play alongside Ian Wright. Competition, of course, is part of the game and I accept the manager's decision. He has only the good of the club at heart and his success proves what a fine job he is making of it.

Although we were a little disappointing in the League this season we still proved we have probably the finest defence in the Championship. The way ahead for us may be to add a little more invention in midfield which could lead to a few more goals.

I know the manager is determined to develop season by season. Manchester United have set a standard and are worthy champions. But we know we have the resolve and determination to challenge them all the way next season.

Introduction

Optimism always comes with the sunshine of high summer as far as George Graham is concerned and July 1993 was no different as Arsenal prepared at London Colney for a new season.

There was every justification for it: though the side finished a disappointing 10th in the League, their driving efforts to win the two domestic cup competitions had been stirring indeed and had taken them into Europe.

One disquieting note as the team reassembled was the fact there had been so little movement of players through the summer. David O'Leary's departure to Leeds United at the end of a distinguished career had been the notable transfer away, but only Eddie McGoldrick of Crystal Palace had been brought in, for a fee of £1m.

He seemed more of a squad buy than a high profile player and there was still the overwhelming concern as to whether Graham had a creative enough midfield to launch a serious threat on the champions Manchester United. United had won the battle for the signature of Roy Keane, whom Arsenal would have liked, and Kenny Dalglish was also seeking to build in preparation for a serious assault on the Championship. Ian Wright, however, who had scored seven goals in the pre-season matches, appeared to be in electrifying form.

The first day it all turned sour. Coventry City raised the curtain on a new Highbury season before a crowd of 26,397 and spanked Arsenal 3-0 in the most surprising result of the opening day.

But matters quickly improved and a draw at Blackburn on September 1, thanks to Kevin Campbell's first League goal of the season, elevated Arsenal to second place where they stayed after defeating Ipswich 4-0, with a hat-trick from Campbell. It was a good warm-up for their first tie in Europe, at home to Odense, and, though Wright and Paul Merson scored in a 2-1 victory, it was not as convincing a performance as Graham might have wished to launch his European campaign.

Defeat by Manchester United later in the month was a disappointment, but the visit to Huddersfield in the Coca-Cola Cup was recuperative, Ian Wright getting his first hat-trick of the season in a 5-0 victory. Another 1-0 victory the following Saturday against

Southampton at Highbury, thanks to Merson, sent the Gunners to their return game against Odense. There was a limited amount of nail-biting before the passage to the second round was safely negotiated with a Campbell goal in a 1-1 draw.

Yet it was in the next spell of League matches that Arsenal slipped badly in the Premiership race. A run of four successive 0-0 draws, two at home and two away, followed by a 2-1 home defeat by Aston Villa was a serious loss of 11 points.

There were consolations. Huddersfield were dispatched from the Coca-Cola Cup and in the third round Arsenal won a replay against Norwich with a draw at Carrow Road. They also performed superbly at home to Standard Liege in the second-round first leg of the Cup Winners' Cup. They performed even better in Belgium where a 7-0 victory without Wright was little short of astonishing.

Arsenal's progress in the Coca-Cola Cup was halted when they surrendered the trophy to an Aston Villa side who went on to win it. It was Villa's second victory at Highbury in a month. The defeat brought to an end a 25-match unbeaten cup run for the Gunners.

Over Christmas there was the bonus not only of three straight wins, against Swindon, Sheffield United and Wimbledon, but of a hatful of goals, a four and two threes. Campbell hit six of them, Wright three and a rare one came from midfield, scored by Ray Parlour.

So on January 3 Arsenal went to QPR 16 points adrift from Manchester United but only two behind second club Blackburn. Again, however, a run of draws finally put them too far away from the leading pair. This time there were six in a row, two 0-0 and the rest 1-1, and, though the team still occupied third place at the end of the sequence, they were drifting further out of the race.

In the middle of that spell they did have the diversion of beginning their defence of the FA Cup at Millwall and a tight game it was. Only an injury-time header by skipper Tony Adams saw the Gunners through but it was a difficult game negotiated.

The long draw sequence ended with a satisfying home win over Blackburn, again by the only goal. Fans were becoming so used to the scoreline they had taken up their now famous chant "One-nil to the Ars-en-al". The supplier this time was Paul Merson.

In the meantime Arsenal had lost their defence of the FA Cup to Bolton Wanderers. It was time, now, to resume the quest for the Cup Winners' Cup after the mid-winter break. That FA Cup exit made winning all the more important since it now seemed the only route to Europe for the 1994-95 season.

A 0-0 draw in Turin on March 2 was a fine result. Arsenal had performed with discipline in the stadium where England's 1990 World Cup hopes had foundered and it was a measure of their defensive excellence that they could bring the Italians back to Highbury with the chance to make home advantage count.

Adams, so often the Highbury hero, excelled even by his own towering standards. He was ably assisted by the equally commanding Steve Bould. Nothing the talented Italian forwards could fling at Arsenal moved these two defenders and, with Paul Davis scheming brilliantly, Arsenal probed for the breakthrough. It was Davis's free-kick, floated in, that drifted tantalisingly away from goalkeeper Giovanni Galli for Adams to steer his side into the semi-final.

The first leg of the semi-final against Paris St Germain was staged in the Parc Des Princes on March 29 and the Gunners knew that if they were to reach the final, they had to come away from Paris with at least a draw – and preferably an away goal.

The result, therefore, was perfect. A 1-1 draw, with Wright scoring the crucial goal, suited them fine. Yet once again in the return leg at Highbury they needed all their resolve and the acumen of Graham to steer them through. A goal from Campbell in the fifth minute was to be decisive but the celebrations were somewhat muted by a booking for Wright for a two-footed tackle which put him out of the final and set the tears flowing.

But Arsenal were through and everything else in their season, the remaining League matches, meant little set against the final in Copenhagen against the Italian holders Parma. Well over 15,000 fans made the journey to Denmark to see a game in which Arsenal started as the underdogs. They had crippling losses: Wright suspended, Jensen, Hillier and Keown all injured. But they performed heroically.

Once again the tactical brilliance of Graham surfaced as Arsenal dealt stealthily with the threat from Parma's exceptional forwards, Colombian Faustino Asprilla, Sweden's Tomas Brolin and Italy's own Gianfranco Zola.

The final was decided on a brilliant goal scored by Alan Smith in the 19th minute. The pass was supplied by Lee Dixon and Smith controlled it superbly before striking a left-foot shot against the upright and across the line.

If Arsenal did not touch the heights in the final, then at least the goal was worthy of the occasion and when Adams received the trophy from Lennart Johansson, the president of Uefa, it placed an approving seal on a season that was disappointing on the domestic front but triumphant in the arena where English football most needed it.

The History of Arsenal FC

Think of Arsenal and more than any other club in the Football League you think of traditional values, continuity, steadfastness.

Manchester United may have usurped them as the most famous English club worldwide through the tragedy of Munich and the exploits of Charlton, Best and Law. Liverpool may have strung together the most outstanding series of results throughout the Seventies and Eighties.

But the aura of Arsenal remains: the marbled halls of Highbury, the bust of the great Herbert Chapman, the era of seeming invincibility.

It is that Chapman age, the Thirties, which is used as the yardstick to judge subsequent achievements. Since his day Arsenal have had nine managers: George Allison, Tom Whittaker, Jack Crayston, George Swindin, Billy Wright, Bertie Mee, Terry Neill, Don Howe and George Graham.

Allison and Whittaker, particularly, continued Chapman's work. But, although Mee memorably won the Double in 1970-71, it is only since the advent of Graham that Arsenal have been truly great again over a sustained period.

Graham, a member of Mee's Double team, took over in May 1986 after a spell at Millwall. The following year Arsenal won the League Cup. Championships followed in 1989 and 1991 plus the League Cup and FA Cup double in 1993. The glory days were back and it was fitting success for Graham who has become a voracious collector of Arsenal memorablia.

Graham, as much as chairman Peter Hill-Wood or any other Arsenal aficionado, understands the meaning of Arsenal, the club's role in the game, its history...and its future.

It all began in 1886 when they were founded in Woolwich and played on Plumstead Common in south east London under the name of Dial Square in a set of red shirts donated by Nottingham Forest. The name was changed to Royal Arsenal, then to Woolwich Arsenal, under which banner they turned professional and entered the League. They became The Arsenal in 1913 and finally, simply, Arsenal.

They had became London's first First Division side in 1904 when they finished second in Division Two and were promoted along with Preston. Still based south of the Thames, they maintained a respectable position in the upper echelons until a disastrous season, 1912-13, when they took only 18 points from a possible 76, finished bottom and were relegated.

It proved a blessing in disguise because it prompted one of the

The sign of the Gunners at the Highbury Stadium

most influential men of those embryonic football times to make a decision which was to affect Arsenal dramatically . Enter Sir Henry Norris a tall, thin, domineering man with large bull-terrier features and a white walrus moustache.

Norris was chairman of Fulham, whom he had taken to two successive Southern League championships and then into the League in 1907. In 1910 he and William Hall had also become directors of Arsenal and until 1913 they effectively controlled both clubs.

Now Norris, who was making a fortune in property deals, recognised that by being in Plumstead, some ten miles from the centre of London, Arsenal were living with the constant threat of small crowds and poor resources. But what about a club situated within minutes of the bright lights of the capital with all its catchment area and financial muscle?

Norris secured a site at Highbury and used his considerable influence to persuade the Arsenal officials to up sticks and head for the north of London, much to the annoyance of Tottenham Hotspur who suddenly found a competitor on their doorstep. Tottenham would have more cause for complaint a few years later.

Arsenal celebrated the opening of their new Highbury Stadium in 1913 by beating Leicester Fosse 2-1 but then, still in the Second Division, found themselves interrupted by the First World War.

By the end of the war Sir Henry Norris was in a fix. He had ploughed £125,000 into Arsenal since 1910, had taken the club to a new stadium at Highbury and then seen the war rob him of any chance to recover even a small part of his investment.

As a result Arsenal were £60,000 in debt, a huge amount when one considers that the highest transfer fee then was less than £3,000.

Norris needed success for his club and needed it quickly. His opportunity came on February 22, 1919 when the Football League Management Committee recommended the extension of the First Division by two clubs.

The move was initiated to allow Chelsea to retain their First Division status. They had been relegated in the final season before the war but it had subsequently been proved that Manchester United, who finished a point above them, had been involved in a rigged game against Liverpool. There was no question that United were guilty as a club, only some of their players, so they were allowed to remain in the First Division.

Chelsea were voted back into the First Division and, with Derby and Preston being promoted by right, that left the question of who would be the 22nd club?

Tottenham were the obvious choice. They had finished bottom of the First Division and precedent was in their favour. Expansion programmes in 1898 and 1905 had seen the two bottom clubs stay up. It seemed simple, but not with Sir Henry Norris around.

As Simon Inglis explains in *The Official Centenary History of the Football League* (Willow Books 1988), Norris launched an amazing and unscrupulous campaign to gain Arsenal that remaining slot.

By 1918 he had become a Coalition Unionist MP for Fulham East, where he was already mayor. Thus he outshone all fellow club chairmen and members of the Management Committee who, for all their powers, had not a fraction of his wealth or influence.

First he threatened a London breakaway. Then, apparently under his bidding, the widely read *Athletic News* commented that Spurs should not stay up. Instead, said the newspaper, promotion should be given to Arsenal as "the oldest league club" who had been most loyal, who now faced financial difficulties and who had "after all only just missed promotion in 1914 on goal difference". All these factors seemed to weigh more heavily than the fact that Arsenal had managed only fifth place in 1915.

Athletic News continued to support Arsenal's cause right up until March 10, 1919, when a Special General Meeting was held, again at the Grand Hotel, Manchester, to discuss the matter.

There was no objection to the expansion programme, the Committee's proposal for two divisions of 22 clubs each being carried unanimously. It was at the next stage that controversy arose – controversy which would have repercussions for years to come and for which no definite explanation has yet been found.

In short, the League appeared to break with all tradition on that

March afternoon in 1919 by electing Arsenal rather than Tottenham to the First Division. As far as we know this is what happened.

Once the clubs had rubber-stamped Chelsea's restoration, the Management Committee proposed that one club be elected from the Second Division to even up the numbers. Crucially the Committee did not offer the clubs a chance to discuss or even vote upon the best method of choosing this 22nd club, as might have been expected. The committee simply made it an open vote, which suggests they were well prepared for a club other than Tottenham to win majority support.

Nevertheless, Tottenham were still in by far the strongest position. Although they had hardly set the First Division alight since being promoted after their debut League season in 1908/1909, they had at least avoided relegation until 1915. Their greatest achievement had been to win the FA Cup in 1901 while members of the Southern League. It was true that their ground at White Hart Lane had been in considerable disarray during the war, with industry taking up one stand and most of the pitch, but by March 1919 the damage was healing and would certainly be repaired in time for the 1919-20 season.

For their part Arsenal's record was reasonable if not spectacular. Relegated in 1913, the year they arrived as unpopular intruders on Tottenham's doorstep, they had just missed promotion on goal average in 1914 and in 1915 finished in fifth place above Birmingham and Hull on goal average but seven points behind Preston in second place.

Of their 22 seasons in the League Arsenal had spent 12 in the lower division and, unlike Spurs, had no major honour to their name. But they had a weapon far mightier than trophies or tradition. They had Sir Henry Norris.

In the *Official Centenary History of Arsenal* (Hamlyn 1986) Phil Soar describes Norris's strategy as the "single most outrageous enterprise ever to be conceived in the history of English football." His aim, said Soar, was to talk The Arsenal back into the First Division by canvassing club chairmen and influential men in the game, by showing "remarkable stealth and political judgment" and, one might add, by offering handsome inducements.

Another Arsenal chronicler, former manager Leslie Knighton, wrote of Norris: "His influence was enormous. He would speak to an important person suggesting a favour, remind a certain financier who was interested that he had once done him a good turn and been promised something in return."

Above all Norris had a great ally in the person of his friend, the League president, "honest" John McKenna. Sir Henry had done the League a very good turn during the war.

In 1916 clubs were asked to contribute one per cent of their gate receipts to keep the League afloat. Because the London clubs were then outside the League's jurisdiction there was no compulsion upon them to pay that levy. But Sir Henry insisted that Arsenal would contribute and was said to have persuaded the four other League clubs in London to do likewise. This gesture of solidarity came at a vital time for the League and once the war was over Norris did not hesitate to remind the League of what had happened.

In his League Centenary book Inglis sets the scene at the March 1919 meeting in Manchester to see which club won First Division status. Of those clubs nominated, the least hopeful were Nottingham Forest who finished the 1914-15 season third from bottom of the Second Division. Surprisingly Forest received three votes. Hull City (seventh in 1915) won one vote (their own), Birmingham (sixth in 1915) polled two, Wolves (fourth in 1915) received four and Barnsley (third in 1915) managed five. The remaining votes were split between the two North London rivals, Tottenham and Arsenal.

At that point the president McKenna, threw his weight behind Arsenal's claim. In an astonishing speech he asserted that Arsenal should be given the remaining First Division place because of their service to the League and their longevity. On both counts he was patently twisting the facts to support his friend Norris.

In terms of "service" it is true that during the war Arsenal had been loyal in contributing to the league and its related charities, but so had dozens of other clubs. On an individual level only one Arsenal official had been active in League affairs – G. H. Leavey, who sat on the Management Committee from 1901-4. So if "service" was a criterion in winning promotion, Second Division clubs like Orient and Forest were just as, if not more, deserving.

McKenna's second assertion that Arsenal had been members longer than Spurs was true. But Wolves, who finished above Arsenal in 1915, had been founder members. So why not elect them?

The simple answer was that none of these clubs had a chairman like Norris. When the votes were counted Tottenham had pooled eight votes, Arsenal 18. Had Spurs been better prepared they might have beaten Arsenal. Instead Norris was the winner.

The real loser was the League, not Spurs. However one massages the facts of the case, the result is the same: the president, the committee and the clubs had succumbed to a rich and powerful politician and property dealer. Current critics of the League may decry the present-day influence of such men in football but never has the League been so manipulated as it was in 1919.

Soar suggests that McKenna's backing was the deciding factor. Once clubs saw that the president "was prepared to support so unlikely a cause", they might have assumed there were sound reasons for Arsenal's promotion: favours to be gleaned in Parliament, gifts to the League...no one ever put a name to the potential benefits. People simply accepted McKenna's judgment.

If financial inducements were offered to individual clubs nothing has been proved, there are no surviving documents to provide clues and, although Norris was later banned from football in 1926, for financial irregularities in 1919, it could well be that his personality was sufficient to sway opinion.

"Everyone was afraid of Sir Henry," remembered Knighton. "And no wonder! I have never met his equal for logic, invective and ruthlessness against all who opposed him."

Thus Arsenal won promotion in the Football League on influence rather than merit but to their credit, having reached the First Division, they have never left it – an unbroken spell unmatched by any other club.

Tottenham, fired by the injustice of it all, won the Second Division Championship in record fashion in 1920 and the FA Cup in 1921. In both 1921 and 1922 they finished above Arsenal. Arsenal's progress remained unspectacular until Norris produced the greatest of his master-strokes, and this time it was legal, above board and utterly inspired. He appointed Herbert Chapman as manager, the man to whom Arsenal owe most of their history and standing in the game.

Herbert Chapman

No manager will ever again have the scope that Chapman had, nor conditions so conducive to his kind of autocratic control, nor, perhaps, his insight into the way to win football matches.

On the field of play the system that Chapman devised became the norm for 30 years. But it was not only on the park that Chapman showed football the way of the future. In Tom Whittaker, appointed in February 1927, he found and encouraged the first of the genuine physiotherapists. In Highbury he built the best club ground in Britain. In advocating floodlights, numbered shirts, white balls and goal judges, independent time-keepers (he installed a 45-minute clock at Highbury only to have it banned by the FA), savings schemes for the players and supporters' trains, he was way ahead of his time. His influence extended everywhere. He changed the old style of strip acquired from Nottingham Forest to give Arsenal players a distinctive look and introduced blue and white socks so that players could distinguish each other in a mêlée (not, as he kidded, because red runs in the wash).

But Chapman was not regarded as a godsend by the ultra-conservative administrators of the day. The Football League thought white balls a ridiculous idea and condemned his campaign for numbering players' shirts as a " stunt" . He tried to get the League to limit transfer fees (many were convinced the game was facing ruin even then) and, when it refused, went out and paid a record for David Jack, the first transfer to top £10,000.

These were days when major clubs were happy to meander along, appointing an old player as secretary-manager, reaching the odd semi-final here, the top five of the League there, letting the senior players run the team. That was success, that was football.

Chapman came from another world, in fact another generation. He was the first true professional in a world of amateurs. The remarkable thing about Chapman, even in comparison with Busby, Revie, Shankly and Paisley whose managerial achievements are not out of proportion with his own, is that his influence extended far beyond the game itself. Probably his greatest achievement off the field is still visible to the millions who travel on London's Piccadilly Line. There, sandwiched between Finsbury Park and Holloway Road, is Arsenal underground station – not Gillespie Road, as the London Transport board had originally called the stop, nor Highbury Hill, a compromise suggestion later put forward, but plain, unadorned Arsenal. Chelsea are on the doorstep of Fulham Broadway station, West Ham next door to Upton Park. What more needs to be said about the powers of persuasion of this remarkable man?

Chapman's eventual success was all the more spectacular following, as it did, a relatively undistinguished playing career with Grimsby, Swindon, Northampton, Sheffield United (where he was a first team regular), Notts County and Tottenham. In 1907 Chapman stumbled into management back with Northampton Town, applying after the Spurs centre-half Walter Bull had turned the job down. Within two years Northampton were Southern League champions but in 1912 Chapman was to return to his native West Riding (he was born at Kiveton Park in 1875) as manager of Second Division Leeds City.

They had a successful spell through the First World War,

winning the Wartime Championship play-off in 1918. But Chapman suffered with the club when they were unceremoniously thrown out of the League in 1919 for refusing to open their books when accused of making illegal payments to their players.

Chapman was suspended for a year, then joined Huddersfield Town, as manager in September 1920. Chapman galvanised the Yorkshire club. In 1924 they won their first championship, albeit on goal average from Cardiff. (In the final game of the season Cardiff were awarded a penalty against Birmingham; after several players had declined to take it Len Davies stepped forward…and missed. Had he scored Cardiff would have been champions for the only time in their history.)

The next year Huddersfield won again with a defensive record for a 42-match season of only 28 goals conceded and they went on to the hat-trick in 1926. By then, however, Chapman had gone. He had achieved all he could in that relatively small wool town. No matter how successful they were, Huddersfield could never become the club of lasting greatness which Chapman sought. The town was too small, too remote, too devoted to rugby league and, thus, too poor. Arsenal, 20 minutes from the bright lights of Piccadilly in the biggest city in the world offered enormous potential. And they had yet to claim a League championship. To take Arsenal to greatness would be to tap the support of millions and to build the kind of monument his talent deserved.

No club could have failed to be impressed by Chapman's remarkable record at Huddersfield in the face of small crowds, little money and the rival code. He had few outstanding players. Alex Jackson, later of the 1928 Wembley Wizards, was the key and played all over the park, and the ex-Aston Villa captain Clem Stephenson, who had won a Cup winner's medal with Villa in 1913 and 1920, provided the experience. The full-backs Barkas and Wadsworth were largely responsible for Huddersfield's magnificent defensive record.

In the three seasons between their Cup win in 1922 and Chapman's departure in 1925 the Huddersfield defence conceded 101 goals in 137 Cup and League games. They were also the first side to go through a 42-match First Division season without having more than two goals scored against them in a game and they set a remarkable record of avoiding defeat in 18 consecutive away matches.

The Arsenal of 1925 were by no means the Arsenal of 1994. Since creeping into the First Division in those most unsavoury circumstances in 1919, Arsenal had proved no great revolutionary force in the First Division and were no better than adequate before Chapman's arrival. Fortunately, however, this date coincided with the most important change the game has seen this century: namely the change in the offside law on June 12, 1925 when the "fewer than three players between the attacker and the goal" was changed to "fewer than two".

Results were startling. In the 1924-25 season, the final one prior to the change in the law, 1,192 goals were scored in the First Division. In the next season that figure rose to 1,703, an increase of nearly 50 per cent or, more graphically, an extra goal for every match played.

But while the immediate result was to move the advantage from defence to attack, the long-term effect was probably negative for the tactical result was, at its simplest, that one attacker became a defender. Credit for devising the third-back game, as it became known, has never been adequately apportioned, but folklore has it that the man behind the innovation was Herbert Chapman.

Almost Chapman's first action on joining Arsenal had been to acquire a scheming inside-forward. The choice was Charlie Buchan, then aged 34 from Sunderland, the man the selectors said was "too clever" to play for England. The fee was an imaginative £2,000 down and £100 for every goal he scored in the subsequent season. Buchan scored 19 in the League and two in the Cup. But it was a transfer significant beyond its immediate impact and unusual terms.

In 1926 Sir Henry Norris, Arsenal's chairman, sued the FA for libel after he had been suspended for making illegal payments. The Buchan case was particularly mentioned and it was shown that Buchan had been offered other inducements to join Arsenal. Norris lost his case and far more, for when he died in 1934 he was an exile from football and also from Arsenal, the club he had dragged from obscurity.

Buchan had walked out on Arsenal before the war over 11 shillings (55p) expenses. His return was to prove inspirational, though not instantly. In one of his first matches, Arsenal were defeated 7-0 at Newcastle on October 3, 1925.

Buchan was so upset at such a humiliating return to the North-East that he and Chapman organised an immediate tactical discussion. One or the other (accounts vary) proposed that Arsenal's centre-half Jack Butler should adopt a purely defensive role and that one of the inside-forwards should drop back to supply the creative link between defence and attack that the centre-half could no longer provide.

Newcastle's centre-half Charlie Spencer claimed he had played just such a defensive role in that vital match and Arsenal's plan may have come from observing Newcastle's success.

Before 1925 the centre-half performed exactly the function his title implied, playing in the middle of the field, helping in defence and instigating attacks.

Buchan expected to be given the creative inside-forward's job himself but Chapman valued his goalscoring abilities too highly and detailed a reserve inside-forward, Andy Neil, to perform the midfield role at Upton Park two days later.

Arsenal won 4-0 with Buchan scoring twice. Chapman gradually revised his team by pushing the full-backs out to mark the wingers and using both his wing-halves now free from their close marking duties to perform midfield roles along with the withdrawn inside-forward. The scheme worked well enough – but was not perfected until Chapman bought the vital creative link, Alex James from Preston in 1929. Thus the team played in a formation which could loosely be described as 3-4-3 or 3-3-4 rather than the 2-3-5 of earlier times.

Alex James signs for Arsenal

Chapman had to find the right players to fit his tactics. His ability was in choosing and moulding those players as parts of a whole. At Huddersfield he inherited a good side, having to buy only Stephenson to make it truly effective. At Arsenal he found a mediocre team – their League positions since reaching the First Division had been 10th , 9th, 17th, 11th, 19th and 20th – and it took several years to create the blend that is remembered today.

The vital stopper centre-half was quickly found, "Policeman" Herbie Roberts arriving from Oswestry for £200. Right-back Tom Parker was signed from Southampton to act as Chapman's captain. His successor as captain, Eddie Hapgood, came for £750 from Kettering where he had spent his time outside football working in a dairy. Hapgood's full-back and England partner George Male was converted from an undistinguished half-back already on Arsenal's books.

Chapman's approach was again a subtle combination of buying, finding and bringing through the ranks. When he thought he had the right man he was unstoppable. David Jack replaced Buchan in 1928, having commanded the first five-figure fee (£10,890) and Alex James arrived in 1929 from Preston for £9,000. This was a remarkable acquisition, helped by the promise of a job as a football demonstrator in Selfridge's, in that Preston had reportedly turned down £15,000 from Manchester City. James was arguably the best player of his day and Chapman set him to work as the crucial midfield link. It took some time to persuade the little Scot to play that role; at Preston he had been a true inside-forward, scoring 53 goals in 147 games.

Life at Highbury was rather more serious – James openly confessed to regarding Second Division football as fun – but he eventually learned to conform, bringing the ball out of defence and spreading those long passes inside the full-backs for wingers Hulme and Bastin.

Bastin was another celebrated example of Chapman's acumen. He had played only 17 games for Third Division Exeter when Chapman bought him for £2,000 as a true goalscoring winger. His 33 goals in the 1932-33 season stand as a record for a conventional winger.

Norris, like most football club chairmen, had his prejudices. He disliked small players and large transfer fees, so imposed a maximum of £1,000 on any purchase. His advertisement for a new manager in the *Athletic News* (to which it was assumed Chapman had responded although in truth Norris had approached him direct) read..."anyone whose sole ability to build up a good side depends

Cliff Bastin

on the payment of heavy and exorbitant transfer fees should not bother to apply".

In Chapman, however, Norris had met his match and the manager simply ignored the chairman's instructions. Success followed. At the end of his first season, 1925-26, Chapman's Arsenal were League runners up to Huddersfield, who completed the League hat-trick Chapman had set them on course for. It was as high as a London club had finished. The great days had begun.

The following year Arsenal were at Wembley, there to lose the only final to be won by a non-English club. Cardiff City's Hugh Ferguson scored with a long speculative shot which goalkeeper Dan Lewis fumbled and then seemed to throw over his own goal-line. Sheen on his new jersey was blamed and the club has made a point of washing new goalkeepers' jerseys before use ever since. In 1928 and 1929 Arsenal finished 10th and 9th in the League. And then in 1930 came a match that was to prove definitive in English football.

Martin Tyler, in *The Story of Football* (Marshall Cavendish 1976), says the future of English football for the next 20 years was contained in the 1930 Cup final, the game which provided Arsenal with their first major honour. To achieve it they beat Huddersfield Town 2-0. Alex James controversially scored the first after taking a quick free kick and a return from Cliff Bastin while the Huddersfield defence protested their unreadiness. Centre-forward Jack Lambert

scored the second.

Such are the facts about a game that summed up a soccer generation in a way that no game had ever done before or is ever likely to do again. As a microcosm of football in the inter-war era it is also easily remembered as the Graf Zeppelin final, Germany's giant airship dipping low over Wembley, a portent between two World Wars. Similarly memorable was the close relationship between the teams: they took the field together (the first time this had happened) and shared a banquet in the evening.

But this game went way beyond simple statistics. It heralded the start of the Arsenal era and the Huddesfield decline. It also signalled the flowering of Chapman's tactical revolution which would dominate English soccer for a decade.

It was Arsenal's first major trophy. They were on the verge of greatness. For Huddersfield it was the final gesture of a glorious decade. The following year Arsenal won their first Championship with 66 points, a record that stood until Leeds United bettered it by one in 1969.

The next year, 1932, Arsenal lost the "over the line" final involving one of Wembley's most disputed goals. Richardson, the Newcastle inside-right, had chased a long pass which seemed to have crossed the goal-line when he reached it. He centred it, nonetheless, and centre-forward Allen flicked it home. Hapgood, who had been marking Richardson, had run across the line when he believed the ball had gone out. What pictorial evidence there was, and those in line, seemed to support Arsenal but the game had swung at that point and the Gunners were not to recover. Less than a year later they lost another Cup game at Walsall which was to become cherished as one of the great Cup shocks of all time.

For Walsall it was all about honour. The 1930s were, for provincial Britain, the worst decade for almost a century. Unemployment had touched three million and in some textile, mining and shipbuilding towns half the workforce was on the dole for years on end. To these towns, with their fierce emotional commitment to football as one of few sources of local pride still available, Arsenal had come to represent the wealth, affluence and unfair advantage that London, still relatively unaffected by unemployment, seemed to have stolen from the rest of the country. Arsenal were the symbol of the South – rich, mean and successful. And in those days there was no television to say that it was not so; all they had was word of mouth and a once-a-year visit from Lucky Arsenal.

That was the cry that rang out across a decade. Time after time Arsenal seemed happy to absorb the pressures of less talented teams and win games away from home by the expedience of a breakaway goal. It was difficult to convince aging boardrooms or the unsophisticated on the terraces that 80 minutes of unrewarded pressure was less valuable than a goal from a sudden break by Hulme or Bastin. Arsenal played a smash-and-grab game – a quick ball inside the full-back from James to Bastin and back to London with the points.

Not that Arsenal were negative at Highbury. In 1930-31, for instance, they scored 127 League goals. But when Arsenal arrived at Third Division Walsall on January 14, 1934, Chapman was not without his problems. Left-back Hapgood, left-half Bob John and two centre-forwards Lambert and Coleman were down with flu, while Hulme was off form and not considered.

As a result Chapman played four virtual unknowns, left-back Tommy Black, outside-right Billy Warnes, centre-foward Charlie Walsh and half-back Norman Sidey – the only one with any first team experience and that limited to one game. The other seven, however, were all internationals including James, Jack and Bastin.

Tyler says in *The Story of Football* that it is unlikely Chapman underestimated the opposition even if the press took delight in pointing out that Arsenal had paid more for their boots that season than the whole Walsall side had cost in transfer and signing-on fees.

Walsall had drawn three of their previous four games and lost the other 5-0. Arsenal, for their part, were probably at their peak. Three weeks earlier, on December 24, 1932, they had produced probably their best performance of the decade by defeating Sheffield United 9-2 at Highbury. Lambert had scored five and Arsenal had gone six points clear at the top of the division, a huge margin in the days of two points for a win.

Chapman, understandably felt that his reserves, with a first-team place to play for, would fight as hard as Walsall. It did not work out that way. Walsh, recruited from amateur soccer, was so nervous that he put his boots on before his socks, missed several easy chances, including the best of the game when he met a centre with his shoulder instead of his head, and had an all-round wretched match. Warnes did not enjoy the hard tackling and Black sealed Arsenal's fate by giving away a penalty in the second half.

For an hour the Gunners survived and, despite the pressure, were beginning to breathe more easily: no score and the prospect of a Highbury replay. Then it happened. Walsall won a corner, Lee centred and Alsop headed home. Sheppard's penalty followed after Black's foul on Alsop, and the great Arsenal were out.

Chapman reacted, probably over-reacted. Poor Walsh was transferred to Brentford within a fortnight and had to carry the ghost of the game throughout his career. Warnes soon went to Norwich and Black seems to have been banned from visiting Highbury again. He was sent straight home from Euston and transferred to Plymouth a week later.

The aftermath of the Walsall game revealed a lesser known side of Chapman – his rigid authoritarianism. He was allowed to rule the club with a rod of iron. On one celebrated occasion he sacked his trainer (and replaced him with Whittaker) for supposedly coaching from the touchline, a duty Chapman reserved for himself.

Walsall were knocked out in the next round, 2-0 by Manchester City, and the freak result had no lasting effect on Arsenal who went on to win the first part of their League hat-trick.

Chapman was not there to see the ultimate success. Within a year of that traumatic day at Walsall, he was dead. It was January 1934 and Arsenal were, typically, top of the First Division. Chapman caught a cold, went to watch a third-team game at Guildford one Wednesday, retired to bed that night and died on the morning of Arsenal's next game against Sheffield Wednesday on the Saturday. The match, according to a report at the time, was "played by weeping players before a weeping crowd".

In 1936 Arsenal unveiled the bust of Chapman in the main hall of the lush new Highbury stand commemorating the anniversary of his death with two minutes' silence and the laying of flowers and a wreath.

After Chapman's death the radio commentator George Allison took over, sensibly leaning on the real team manager, trainer Tom Whittaker, and his assistant Joe Shaw. New players were in the tough Chapman mould – half-back Jack Crayston and centre-forward Ted Drake, who remains the holder of a First Division record with his seven goals from eight shots in a League game against Aston Villa.

Even as they declined, unconvincingly winning the Cup with another Drake goal in 1936 and the Championship with only 52 points in 1938, the outstanding England international inside-forward Raich Carter could say of them: "They were not merely a great side, they towered so much above every other club. We were in total awe of them."

By that time only Hapgood, Male and Bastin survived from Chapman's great team. Even James retired that year to run his corner shop and died at the early age of 51 from cancer.

The Second World War treated Arsenal cruelly. It left them effectively without a side. Ten of the team who had played their last League game in 1939 were unavailable when normal peace-time football resumed in 1946.

Nonetheless they were still a force after the war, as they were after Chapman's death. Having taken two championships under Allison (1934-35, 1937-38) and two more under Whittaker (1947-48 and 1952-53) and won the Cup in 1950.

But then the glory dimmed and progress became satisfactory

Record-breaking goal scorer,
Ted Drake

rather than sensational, although in 1958 they were involved in arguably the greatest League match of all time when they lost 5-4 at Highbury to Matt Busby's Manchester United Babes in their last appearance in England before the Munich disaster.

Managers came and went without suggesting a return to former greatness. Even that golden hero of English soccer, former international captain Billy Wright, failed to produce the team the fans craved. And meanwhile, down the road at Spurs, Arthur Rowe and then Bill Nicholson were working their magic alongside Blanchflower, White and Mackay as Spurs secured the Double and then added the FA Cup again in 1962 and 1967.

Wright was sacked in 1966 after four mainly miserable years in which his best League finish was eighth. Arsenal, controversially, turned to a young physiotherapist called Bertie Mee. He was to reign for 10 years, to win what became the UEFA Cup, Arsenal's first European success, in 1969-70 and then, in 1970-71, to provide Arsenal with a success which even Herbert Chapman had failed to provide: the League and Cup Double.

That season held all the ingredients of a first-class thriller; culminating in cliff-hanging suspense. In a remarkable 64-match campaign, for the last 10 weeks of which they played two matches a week, they won both trophies in the final six days of the season. After an epic struggle with Leeds, they took the Championship in their last match against arch rivals Tottenham at White Hart Lane. And at Wembley they overcame a goal deficit against Liverpool to snatch victory in the last minutes of extra time.

At the beginning of the season Arsenal were no more than promising challengers for honours, having finished only 12th in the League in 1969-70. But they had won the European Fairs Cup, their first major trophy for 17 years. Captained by the veteran Scot Frank McLintock and built round a solid defence, with Bob Wilson out-standing in goal, Arsenal were at an early stage of development. Any suggestion that this young side could bring off the Double would have been dismissed as a flight of fancy.

Before the season , defender Peter Simpson and midfield schemer Jon Sammels sustained serious injuries. And rising star Charlie George broke an ankle in the first match. So three first-choice players were out of the game.

These setbacks brought changes, two of which were to prove sig-nificant. The burly, raw 19-year-old Ray Kennedy took over George's striking role and full-back Peter Storey moved into midfield. Kennnedy had played only twice in Arsenal's League side and had come on as substitute in the last few minutes of the Fairs Cup final, first leg, heading a vital goal. Slow at first, he struck up a fine understanding with John Radford and was to finish as Arsenal's top scorer.

Storey, Arsenal's hard man, was known for his tenacity in the tackle rather than his footballing skills. A great competitor, he relished his new role and was later to be capped by England.

The most significant early match was the home game with Leeds. Champions with a record 67 points two seasons earlier, Leeds had chased League, Cup and European Cup in 1969-70, narrowly failing in each. This season they were looking invincible and had won all five of their opening games. But despite losing Eddie Kelly, sent off after 22 minutes, Arsenal not only held Leeds to a goalless draw but won an equal share of the play.

Of the next 18 games, Arsenal won 14 and drew three. Their sole defeat, an extraordinary 5-0 thrashing at Stoke at the end of September, served as a warning against over-confidence. No team put more than two goals past them again.

By the time Arsenal's League run was brought to an end in mid-January the title chase had developed into a two-horse race. Arsenal, with 38 points from 24 games, had narrowed the gap to one point

Charlie George

and held a game in hand over Leeds. The next side, Spurs, were eight points adrift. But two successive defeats allowed Leeds to open a five-point lead. The critics began to write off Arsenal but they had reckoned without the Gunners' determination...and Charlie George.

Bertie Mee put George in for George Graham in the fourth-round FA Cup replay with Portsmouth. Arsenal were a goal down and struggling when George scored after a 50-yard run. Long-haired, flamboyant, with a deadly shot and almost telepathic passing ability, George stole the limelight. In Arsenal's fifth-round victory in the Maine Road mud he scored both goals, one a mighty free-kick through the Manchester City wall, the other after another long run.

Now every match was a virtual cup final. When Arsenal lost at Derby, Leeds went seven points ahead and, even allowing for two games in hand, Arsenal's League hopes looked bleak.

The turning point came at the beginning of March when Arsenal went to Molineux and gave a glorious display of football in a 3-0 win over fourth-placed Wolves. It was the start of nine straight wins in the League, a run that took them to the top of the table as Leeds began to slip.

Meanwhile Arsenal had reached the semi-final of the Cup but found themselves two down at half-time to unfancied Stoke. Now it was Storey's turn to show his stuff. He hit home a volley soon after the interval and converted a penalty two minutes from time after a Stoke defender had palmed a goalbound McLintock header off the line. Arsenal swept through the replay 2-0.

The run-in to the last, almost unbelievable week was packed with drama. Arsenal went top on April 17 when Leeds lost at home to West Brom in a controversial match and George, having a poor game against Newcastle, suddenly smashed in a brilliant winner. Leeds went back on top when they beat Arsenal at Elland Road with a hotly disputed last-minute goal but Arsenal came back into the running by beating Stoke with a late goal from substitute Kelly.

The scene was set for the final week. Arsenal had to win or draw 0-0 at Spurs on the Monday night to take the title. A capacity crowd of 52,000 at White Hart Lane with almost the same number outside saw Kennedy crown his remarkable first season with the winner two minutes from time.

There was still a Cup final to play – against a rapidly improving Liverpool side with arguably the best defence in the country. Again Arsenal did it the hard way. They made enough chances to have won comfortably but, with no score after 90 minutes, the game went

Frank McLintock and Bertie Mee celebrate their 1971 League triumph

into extra time.

Steve Heighway broke away on the left and scored for Liverpool after two minutes. It looked all up for the Double. But Arsenal refused to panic and 10 minutes later Kelly, who had come on for Storey, took advantage of a rare defensive slip to equalise. The occasion demanded something special now and George provided it. With eight minutes to go he collected a Radford pass, slashed a 20-yard drive past Ray Clemence and then sprawled backwards on the Wembley turf in delight.

McLintock, who had been voted Footballer of the Year, collected the trophy. Graham, who found Wembley the perfect setting for his classy skills, was voted Man of the Match. Goalkeeper Wilson and all-purpose winger George Armstrong had played in all 64 games.

In the season Arsenal had sometimes played powerful, brilliant football. Frequently they had to rely on teamwork. They had been drawn away in every round of the Cup, yet still found the will to prevail. It was a lesson in professionalism not lost on the young George Graham.

He remembered it well when he came to the Highbury hot seat in May 1986 via a playing career that embraced Aston Villa, Chelsea, Arsenal, Manchester United, Portsmouth and Crystal Palace, as well as 12 Scottish caps. A spell as coach at Palace was followed by a promising managerial debut at Millwall. When Arsenal decided to part company with Don Howe, Graham was a logical, and inspired, choice.

Within a year Arsenal had won the League Cup, beating Spurs in the semi-final after a replay and then seeing off Liverpool 2-1 in the final. Two seasons later Graham steered them, dramatically, to their first Championship for 18 years.

His "new-look" Arsenal had been built around home-grown talent within the club like Tony Adams, David Rocastle, Michael Thomas and Paul Merson supplemented by some shrewd buys: in defence Nigel Winterburn from Wimbledon for £407,000, Steve Bould from Stoke for £390,000 and Lee Dixon, also from Stoke, for £400,000; in attack the target man Alan Smith from Leicester for £800,000 and Brian Marwood, a latter-day if inferior George Armstrong, for £600,000 from Sheffield Wednesday.

In the end, after a nail-biting finale, Arsenal were left needing to win by two goals at Anfield in the final game of the season to take the title and deprive Liverpool of the Double. Smith struck first and then, in the 90th minute, Thomas kept cool amid the hysteria to add the crucial second goal with the sweetest of finishes.

Arsenal's campaign to retain the Championship in 1989-90 began well once they recovered from a 4-1 drubbing by Manchester United on the opening day – and in November they were top. But the signs were not good; few of their victories were comfortable. The 4-3 home defeat of Norwich on the first Saturday in November was particularly uncomfortable. The game marked David O'Leary's 622nd major match for Arsenal, a club record, and it was an eventful occasion. O'Leary scored an equaliser as Arsenal recovered from 3-1 down and was also shown the yellow card. Then a last-minute penalty which gave Arsenal victory sparked a fracas involving 19 players. Three weeks later the FA Disciplinary Committee fined Norwich £50,000 and Arsenal £20,000. It was the first time clubs had been held responsible for their players in such an incident.

Arsenal's wheels wobbled in the fourth round of the Littlewoods

Cup in November. After a two-leg, 8-1 victory over Plymouth and a 1-0 defeat of Liverpool at Highbury, a visit to Second Division Oldham did not seem so awesome. Yet they were beaten 3-1 and, from Christmas onwards, their season fell apart. Five out of six successive away games were lost, with only one goal scored. FA Cup defeat at QPR followed, Rocastle and Thomas suffered dramatic losses in form and the goals dried up for Smith, only 11 compared with his 23 the previous season. On the other hand the introduction of Kevin Campbell was an exciting indication of the future.

Arsenal and Norwich punch it out

Graham acted quickly in the summer to restore Arsenal's fortunes. Swedish international Anders Limpar was imported from Cremonese for £1 million, central defender Andy Linighan joined from Norwich for £1.25 million and, most expensive of all, goalkeeper David Seaman moved across London from Queens Park Rangers for £1.3 million. The Seaman buy illustrated Graham's ruthless streak as he unloaded John Lukic, so instrumental in Arsenal's 1989 Championship, to Leeds for £1 million.

The dramatic transfer activity was mirrored by the events of the following season. A heated exchange on the pitch between Arsenal and Manchester United players during a 1-0 victory at Old Trafford brought a £50,000 fine for both clubs. Arsenal were also deducted two League points, leaving them eight points behind Liverpool. Then their captain Tony Adams was jailed for four months on December 19 at Southend Crown Court for reckless driving after a party. Even with maximum remission for good behaviour Adams would not return to the team until mid-February.

Arsenal nonetheless began their League campaign with 23 unbeaten games and their 2-1 defeat by Chelsea at Stamford Bridge on February 2 turned out to be their only defeat of the League season, a 20th-century record. The Championship was decided on Bank Holiday Monday, May 6. Nottingham Forest, who all those years ago back in 1886 had given the penniless Arsenal club a strip of red shirts, now did them a greater favour by handing them the Championship with a 2-1 defeat of Liverpool at the City Ground. Later that day Arsenal celebrated in style, walloping Manchester United 3-1.

Spurs denied them the Double with victory in the the FA Cup semi-finals but no one doubted George Graham deserved his title of Manager of the Year. In 1993 he was to add the League Cup for a second time and the FA Cup. Another glorious decade seemed to beckon in the ongoing story of Arsenal Football Club.

Arsenal's League Championship team of 1991

The Matches

---

7 August to 7 May

August 7

ARSENAL 1

MANCHESTER UNITED 1

(Half-time score: 1-1)
(United won 5-4 on penalties)

Arsenal: Seaman, Dixon, Winterburn, Davis, Linighan, Adams, Campbell, Wright, Merson, Limpar, Jensen.
Subs: Keown, McGoldrick, Selley, Heaney, Miller.
Man Utd: Schmeichel, Parker, Irwin, Bruce, Pallister, Ince, Kanchelskis, Cantona, Keane, Hughes, Giggs.
Subs: McClair, Ferguson, Sealey, Robson, Sharpe.
Scorers: Arsenal: Wright 40; Man Utd: Hughes 8.
Referee: G Ashby (Worcs)
Attendance: 66,519

Arsenal came into the Charity Shield off a 2-1 defeat by Charlton in a friendly at The Valley. Hardly the recipe for super confidence, it seemed, but in Wembley's wide open spaces they matched Manchester United, 15-8 favourites for the title, all the way.

Alex Ferguson had missed United's 1-0 friendly defeat of Celtic with flu but was back at Wembley to see splendid goals by Mark Hughes and Ian Wright take the pre-season spectacular into a penalty shoot-out. Arsenal goalkeeper David Seaman was elected to take one of the kicks – and his lame attempt was smothered by opposite number Peter Schmeichel.

Arsenal had been listed at 5-1 for the title by the bookies and the reintroduction of Paul Davis to their midfield was a source of optimism for their fans. Davis had endured a period of estrangement with manager George Graham but all that appeared behind them after the gifted 32-year-old celebrated the signing of a new contract with a cultured passing display.

It was a fine, exciting game of ebb and flow until the heat trapped in the stadium tugged at the legs and lungs of footballers shaking off the excesses of a short summer.

United displayed an embarrassment of riches on their substitutes' bench – Bryan Robson, Lee Sharpe and Brian McClair. Arsenal's selection problems were less pressing but £1 million players like Martin Keown and Eddie McGoldrick were left wondering exactly where they would fit in.

Graham was full of praise for strikers Wright and Kevin Campbell. "They can form a great partnership," he said. "I was really pleased with the way Kevin played. He is looking sharp again and just needs a couple of goals to lift his confidence.

"The trouble with a young player like him is that he wins a championship medal at the age of 21 and then has an off-season. I've then got to decide whether to sell or keep him and hope I don't make the wrong decision."

It would be a recurring theme throughout the coming months as Campbell mixed performances of breathtaking power with others of mind-numbing mediocrity.

But the season was young and hopes were high. "When the real ball game begins I think there will be more clubs than ours involved," said Graham. "Sheffield Wednesday and Aston Villa for instance...and it will be tight with a lot of games like this one."

Mark Hughes gives United the lead

August 14

ARSENAL 0

COVENTRY 3
(Half-time score: 0-1)

Arsenal: Seaman, Dixon, Linighan, Adams, Winterburn, Limpar, Jensen (Keown), Davis, Merson (McGoldrick), Wright, Campbell.
Sub: Miller.
Coventry: Gould, Sheridan, Rennie, Atherton, Babb, Robson, Wegerle, Ndlovu, J Williams, Quinn, Flynn.
Subs: Morgan, Harford, Dalton.
Bookings: Coventry: Quinn (dissent), Babb (foul).
Scorer: Coventry: Quinn 34 (pen), 62, 65.
Referee: A Wilkie (Chester Le Street)
Attendance: 26,397

Arsenal started the season as everyone's idea of strong title contenders but found themselves thrown in the opening exchange by a man they call "Sumo".

The rotund figure of Coventry striker Mick Quinn may look more suited to a Sunday league pub team but, at 31, the Premiership's unlikeliest star still nurses a long-standing ambition to play for England.

Highbury this day, he clearly decided, was the right time and place to air those aspirations and he stunned Arsenal with a hat-trick.

The chubby, apparently clumsy Quinn shocked the meanest defence in the country as the Coventry supporters joyously sang: "He's fat, he's round, he scores on every ground."

The delighted Coventry manager Bobby Gould, who snapped up Quinn for £200,000 from Newcastle, said: "I'm not worried about his shape. If you're fat, you're fat. It's what you do on the park that matters. Mick has this predatory instinct and the sort of technique you'd like to teach to every kid. He's been scoring goals throughout his career, yet he still believes he has something to prove."

Quinn's explosive contribution rudely jolted Arsenal who, from a lively first half-hour, had looked to be heading for a comfortable afternoon. Anders Limpar set up close-range efforts for Kevin Campbell and Paul Merson, Nigel Winterburn forced a fine save from Jonathan Gould and an Andy Linighan shot required a goal-line clearance from Stewart Robson.

But once Quinn put Coventry ahead with a 34th-minute penalty following Lee Dixon's block on Peter Ndlovu, Arsenal's commitment faded. "We had a lot of quality players out there but the majority of them didn't live up to their reputations," said manager George Graham.

Quinn, who had backed himself for £50 at 50-1 to finish as the Premiership's top scorer, fired home his second with his left foot after 62 minutes and his third with his right four minutes later to complete the season's first hat-trick.

Arsenal goalkeeper David Seaman confirmed the ferocity of the last two. "I just didn't see the ball," he said. "It was some shooting."

David Seaman dives in vain for Mick Quinn's second goal

August 16

TOTTENHAM 0

ARSENAL 1
(Half-time score: 0-0)

Tottenham: Thorstvedt, Austin, Campbell, Samways, Calderwood, Mabbutt, Sedgley, Howells, Sheringham, Durie, Dozzell.
Subs: Caskey, Hendry, Walker.
Arsenal: Seaman, Keown, Winterburn, Davis, Linighan, Adams, Jensen, Wright, Campbell, McGoldrick, Parlour.
Subs: Selley, Smith, Miller.
Bookings: Spurs: Mabbutt (ungentlemanly conduct), Samways (ungentlemanly conduct), Austin (foul); Arsenal: Wright (ungentlemanly conduct), Parlour (foul), Keown (foul).
Scorer: Arsenal: Wright 87.
Referee: D Elleray (Harrow)
Attendance: 28,355

On the day Ian Wright released a record called "Do The Right Thing", he did exactly that for Arsenal. His 87th-minute goal won a North London derby packed with passion and commitment.

It was no less than Arsenal deserved. After their aberration against Coventry, this was a performance of mean maturity. George Graham acted with typical ruthlesslness, dropping Anders Limpar and Paul Merson. He offered, instead, the more direct Eddie McGoldrick his first League chance with the club and stiffened his midfield with the inclusion of the aggressive and mobile Ray Parlour. The fact that it took Arsenal until the dying embers of the game to fan the flames of their season was due to their own profligacy and a poor refereeing decision.

They should have been awarded a goal in the first half when Tony Adams forced a rebound over the line before Colin Calderwood cleared. Graham said later: "It was so far over the line I'd like to know where the linesman was. Maybe he should watch the video."

But on a night when Wright seemed to turn every touch into a chance it was his class which shone through as Arsenal dominated with fine passing and flowing football. Arsenal almost drew first blood when Parlour whipped a cross in from the right flank and Wright, displaying his lethal speed in a late run, dived at the ball which flashed across the face of Erik Thorstvedt's goal.

Spurs, subdued for the first half-hour, threatened when Adams pushed Teddy Sheringham, who clipped a bending free-kick too high. Sheringham then wasted a better chance when a ball from Jason Dozzell spilled out of David Seaman's hands. As Sheringham shaped for a shooting angle he hesitated too long and was crowded out by Arsenal defenders.

Arsenal seemed to have taken the lead when a McGoldrick free-kick, headed on by Adams, was struck against the post by Wright. As it came back Adams drove the ball towards goal before it was cleared by Calderwood.

Wright's predatory skills proved conclusive three minutes from time when a McGoldrick corner was flicked goalwards by Andy Linighan and Wright neatly deflected it home with his head.

August 21

George Graham lost the week's transfer battle but ended up winning the match. Queens Park Rangers' Andy Sinton chose to join Wednesday for £2.7 million rather than Arsenal and then found himself on the end of a familiar defeat by the Londoners.

Wednesday had lost both the FA Cup and League Cup finals against Arsenal the previous season and this time their manager Trevor Francis was forced to admit, "We deserved to lose today."

Match-winner Ian Wright's partnership with the powerful Kevin Campbell always held a sharper edge than Wednesday's pairing of David Hirst and Paul Warhurst.

Warhurst even finished the game at right-back as Wednesday threw on Mark Bright in a final flurry of desperation. Francis blamed sloppy defending for Arsenal's ninth-minute goal. Campbell carved out the opening to provide Wright with the chance to finish despite the attentions of three defenders.

Arsenal's hungry pair continued to menace Wednesday and Campbell forced excellent saves from Chris Woods. "Kevin was outstanding," said Graham. "We out-passed Wednesday all through and what pleased me most was the manner of our performance. Trevor has a good squad but we won this one easily."

Wednesday came closest in the 29th minute when Hirst finished a chance he had created himself by shooting straight at David Seaman.

SHEFFIELD WEDNESDAY 0

ARSENAL 1
(Half-time score: 0-1)

Sheff Wed: Woods, King, Worthington, Palmer, Pearce, Walker, Sheridan, Hyde, Hirst, Warhurst, Sinton.
Subs: Bart-Williams, Bright, Pressman.
Arsenal: Seaman, Keown, Adams, Linighan, Winterburn, McGoldrick, Jensen, Davis, Parlour (Merson), Wright, Campbell.
Subs: Selley, Miller.
Scorer: Arsenal: Wright 9.
Referee: R Hart (Darlington)
Attendance: 26,023

League Table After Match

	P	W	D	L	F	A	Pts
Liverpool	3	3	0	0	10	1	9
Everton	3	3	0	0	7	2	9
Ipswich	3	3	0	0	5	0	9
Man Utd	3	2	1	0	6	1	7
Coventry	3	2	1	0	6	2	7
Norwich	3	2	0	1	7	4	6
Blackburn	3	2	0	1	5	4	6
Tottenham	3	2	0	1	2	1	6
Arsenal	3	2	0	1	2	3	6
Aston Villa	3	1	2	0	6	3	5
Wimbledon	3	1	2	0	5	3	5
Leeds	3	1	1	1	2	5	4
Sheffield Utd	3	1	0	2	5	8	3
Oldham	3	1	0	2	1	4	3
QPR	3	1	0	2	4	8	3
Chelsea	3	0	1	2	2	4	1
Newcastle	3	0	1	2	2	4	1
Man City	3	0	1	2	1	3	1
West Ham	3	0	1	2	1	4	1
Sheffield Wed	3	0	1	2	0	3	1
Southampton	3	0	0	3	1	5	0
Swindon	3	0	0	3	1	9	0

August 24

Arsenal: Seaman, McGoldrick, Keown, Linighan, Winterburn, Selley, Parlour, Davis (Hillier), Campbell, Wright, Merson.
Subs: Limpar, Miller.
Leeds: Lukic, Kelly, Fairclough, Newsome, Dorigo, Strachan, McAllister, Batty, Whelan, Speed, Deane.
Subs: Wallace, Wetherall, Beeney.
Bookings: Arsenal: Wright (foul); Leeds: McAllister (dissent).
Scorers: Arsenal: Newsome (o.g.) 2, Merson 57; Leeds: Strachan 75.
Referee: K Hackett (Sheffield)
Attendance: 29,042

Paul Merson waltzed back into favour with the Arsenal faithful, scoring one goal and making another, but still found himself out of step with manager George Graham. "I thought he played spasmodically," said Graham. "I know what he is capable of and there is still plenty left."

It was a theme which would recur throughout the season. But at least Merson got a game this time after spending the first three matches on the bench. That was more than could be said for his old buddy David Rocastle, still out of favour at Elland Road, an exile that would end only with his sale to Manchester City at the turn of the year. The ankle injury that kept out Tony Adams was matched by the absence in the Leeds team of Arsenal old boy David O'Leary.

Leeds travelled to Highbury with their appalling away record hanging like a millstone. The last time they had won outside Elland Road was May 1992 and then it was just down the road against Sheffield United in a match which had clinched them the championship.

Their homesickness surfaced again after only 56 seconds. Jon Newsome, who had replaced O'Leary, got off to a traumatic start by gifting Arsenal an own goal. Merson, playing only because John Jensen was on international duty with Denmark, raced down the right wing and hit a cross to the near post. The waiting Kevin Campbell stumbled as he went for the ball which bobbled on to Newsome's knee and spun past the bemused John Lukic.

Leeds battled for the equaliser and almost drew level after 36 minutes of an otherwise sterile first half. A smart move down the left gave Gary Speed the chance to provide a teasing cross towards Brian Deane but the ball struck Martin Keown and went for a corner.

Ian Wright seemed to be a victim of his own reputation when he was booked by Keith Hackett for a foul on Leeds teenager Gary Kelly.

Both sides made changes in the second half, Arsenal to consolidate and Leeds to create. David Hillier replaced Paul Davis for Arsenal while Rod Wallace came on for young Noel Whelan.

There was encouragement for Leeds in the shape of a Gordon Strachan cross from the right which Deane turned on smartly.

Arsenal were fortunate that Keown got a foot to the ball to divert it into the side netting.

Jon Newsome's own goal

Arsenal secured their third win of the season with a second goal after 57 minutes, courtesy of a mistake from Kelly. As Wright hooked the ball into the Leeds area the teenage defender attempted a back header to Lukic. Leeds later complained that Kelly was held by Campbell and certainly the pass was short. Before it could reach the goalkeeper Merson arrived to hook the ball home.

Leeds frustration surfaced with captain Gary McAllister booked for dissent. But they channelled their aggression to create a goal of rare quality from Strachan after 75 minutes. Lukic's long goal-kick was chested into the path of the little Scot by Deane. Strachan collected the ball on his right foot and struck it with his left past Seaman.

"We showed them too much respect after going one up and tended to play too deep," said Graham.

League Table After Match

	P	W	D	L	F	A	Pts
Man Utd.	4	3	1	0	8	2	10
Liverpool	3	3	0	0	10	1	9
Everton	3	3	0	0	7	2	9
Ipswich	3	3	0	0	5	0	9
Blackburn	4	3	0	1	7	4	9
Arsenal	4	3	0	1	4	4	9
Coventry	4	2	2	0	9	5	8
Norwich	3	2	0	1	7	4	6
Tottenham	3	2	0	1	2	1	6
Sheffield Utd.	4	2	0	2	7	9	6
Aston Villa	4	1	2	1	7	5	5
Wimbledon	4	1	2	1	6	5	5
Oldham	4	1	1	2	4	7	4
Leeds	4	1	1	2	3	7	4
QPR	3	1	0	2	4	8	3
Chelsea	3	0	1	2	2	4	1
Newcastle	3	0	1	2	2	4	1
West Ham	3	0	1	2	1	4	1
Sheffield Wed	3	0	1	2	0	3	1
Man City	4	0	1	3	1	5	1
Southampton	3	0	0	3	1	5	0
Swindon	3	0	0	3	1	9	0

August 28

ARSENAL 2

EVERTON 0
(Half-time score: 0-0)

Arsenal: Seaman, Keown, Linighan, Adams, Winterburn, McGoldrick, Parlour, Jensen, Hillier (Merson), Campbell, Wright.
Subs: Selley, Miller.
Everton: Southall, Holmes, Jackson, Ablett, Hinchcliffe, Stuart, Horne, Ebbrell, Ward, Rideout, Cottee.
Subs: Preki, Barlow, Kearton.
Scorer: Arsenal: Wright 48, 78.
Referee: K. Burge (Tonypandy)
Attendance: 29,063

Paul Merson found himself punished, then praised by George Graham. First he was made to sit on the substitutes' bench for 45 minutes, then he was sent on to galvanise his fellow Gunners.

Merson, with an eye to the England World Cup squad being announced by Graham Taylor a couple of days later for the match with Poland, had been complaining that he wanted to play as a striker for Arsenal...so Graham promptly dropped him from his winger's slot.

"He is not Paul Merson of England; he is Paul Merson of Arsenal. He has got to get that into his head," said Graham. "Players have to learn that it is their clubs they play for, first and foremost."

In the event, Merson's replacement David Hillier was injured and could not come out for the second half. "That's life," grinned Graham. "Bertie Mee used to drop me regularly from the Arsenal Double-winning team."

But if Merson had mixed fortunes, another of Taylor's England hopefuls could hardly have performed more impressively. Ian Wright scored the two match-winning goals and both were spectacular even by his electrifying standards.

"What can you do about a player like that?" pleaded Everton manager Howard Kendall. "We badly missed our injured centre-half Dave Watson. We just couldn't cope with Wright, but who could?"

Certainly not Everton goalkeeper Neville Southall despite his customary heroics. Wright looked as if he had been plugged into the Highbury mains and he threw the switch in such dazzling fashion that he earned a sustained standing ovation from the often hard-to-please Arsenal patrons.

The goals came via huge punts from goalkeeper David Seaman and though Wright later credited his striking partner Kevin Campbell with headed flick-on assists the ball must have been a white blur to Southall.

The first goal came in the 48th minute when Wright connected with the ball on the first bounce to send a shot raking under the diving Southall. The second, 30 minutes later, followed a dance routine which would have done credit to Mr Bojangles. Wright transferred the ball from foot to foot before executing an exquisite lob.

Merson had provided a prelude to all this when he came off the bench and immediately struck an upright when it looked easier to score.

Everton had shown little punch up front and Kendall attempted to put this right by pulling off Tony Cottee and Graham Stuart. He could have permed any two from 11 for all the difference it made against the rock-like Arsenal defence.

Kendall might have wished for a Merson in his team to lift them out of the very, very ordinary. "When he came on he started to run riot," Kendall said. "I had to change my side round to account for that."

But Graham was unrepentant about his treatment of Merson. "We have a whole bunch of forwards here and if they are not playing well I will drop them. Paul's response today when he came on was excellent. I made a decision and, if that is the response I get, then I made the right decision. It is no good having talent if you don't use it. You have to work hard. I see it every week in the Italian League. I see world-class players working.

"Ryan Giggs works hard. It is not about talent alone. Paul can work a lot harder. I have been his biggest advocate here when he has fallen out with certain people. But if he is not producing it he'll be out the same as other players."

League Table After Match

	P	W	D	L	F	A	Pts
Man Utd.	5	4	1	0	11	3	13
Liverpool	5	4	0	1	13	3	12
Arsenal	5	4	0	1	6	4	12
Norwich	5	3	1	1	8	4	10
Ipswich	5	3	1	1	6	2	10
Blackburn	5	3	1	1	8	5	10
Coventry	5	2	3	0	10	6	9
Everton	5	3	0	2	7	5	9
Tottenham	5	3	0	2	4	3	9
Aston Villa	5	2	2	1	8	5	8
Sheffield Utd.	5	2	1	2	8	10	7
Wimbledon	5	1	3	1	7	6	6
QPR	5	2	0	3	8	10	6
Chelsea	5	1	2	2	5	5	5
Newcastle	5	1	2	2	4	5	5
Oldham	5	1	2	2	5	8	5
West Ham	5	1	1	3	3	8	4
Leeds	5	1	1	3	3	9	4
Southampton	5	1	0	4	7	9	3
Man City	5	0	2	3	2	6	2
Sheffield Wed	5	0	2	3	1	6	2
Swindon	5	0	1	4	2	14	1

September 1

BLACKBURN 1
ARSENAL 1
(Half-time score: 1-0)

Blackburn: Mimms, Berg, May, Moran, Le Saux, Ripley, Sherwood, Marker, Wilcox, Gallacher, Newell.
Subs: Shearer, Atkins, Talia.
Arsenal: Seaman, Keown, Linighan, Adams, Winterburn, McGoldrick, Jensen, Merson (Selley), Parlour, Campbell, Wright.
Subs: Lydersen, Miller.
Bookings: Arsenal: Adams (foul).
Scorers: Blackburn: Gallacher 36; Arsenal: Campbell 75.
Referee: D Allison (Lancaster)
Attendance: 14,051

League Table After Match

	P	W	D	L	F	A	Pts
Man Utd.	6	5	1	0	14	3	16
Arsenal	6	4	1	1	7	5	13
Liverpool	6	4	0	2	13	4	12
Coventry	6	3	3	0	11	6	12
Norwich	6	3	2	1	11	7	11
Aston Villa	6	3	2	1	9	5	11
Ipswich	6	3	2	1	7	3	11
Blackburn	6	3	2	1	9	6	11
Tottenham	6	3	1	2	5	4	10
Wimbledon	6	2	3	1	8	6	9
Everton	6	3	0	3	7	6	9
QPR	6	3	0	3	10	11	9
Sheffield Utd	6	2	1	3	9	12	7
Leeds	6	2	1	3	4	9	7
Chelsea	6	1	3	2	6	6	6
Newcastle	6	1	3	2	5	6	6
Man City	6	1	2	3	5	7	5
Oldham	6	1	2	3	5	9	5
West Ham	6	1	1	4	3	11	4
Southampton	6	1	0	5	7	10	3
Sheffield Wed	6	0	3	3	4	9	3
Swindon	6	0	1	5	3	17	1

Arsenal maintained their image as a difficult team to beat but they did so at the expense of the good humour of Blackburn manager Kenny Dalglish.

Dalglish was far from impressed by the Tony Adams tackle which left Blackburn goalscorer Kevin Gallacher limping into the dug-out and it sent the former Liverpool and Scotland star into a discourse about the perils of strikers.

"When you are playing well you get a boot," said Dalglish, with obvious feeling. "Mike Newell, Alan Shearer and David Hirst played well last year and they copped it. Kevin was playing well tonight and he copped it. You can't argue with that consistency."

Gallacher had deservedly put his side ahead with a brilliantly taken goal eight minutes before half-time. The move began deep in the Blackburn half at the feet of Henning Berg. The Norwegian defender, celebrating his 24th birthday, hit a stunning pass down the right. It allowed Newell to sweep round Adams and find Gallacher, who was too quick for Linighan and too accurate for the diving Seaman. The Arsenal goalkeeper, plunging to his right, made contact with Gallacher's angled shot but had no hope of keeping it out.

Blackburn should have been two up a minute later but Jason Wilcox contrived to fire wide from a glittering chance teed up by Stuart Ripley. Alan Shearer, Blackburn's £3.3 million striker being nursed back after two knee operations, was substitute for the fifth successive game. But Adams's crude challenge on Gallacher, which earned the Arsenal captain a booking, announced Shearer's 53rd-minute entrance.

It was Arsenal, though, who scored in the 75th minute when Campbell raced on to Eddie McGoldrick's long pass, side-stepped David May and beat Bobby Mimms at his near post.

Arsenal manager George Graham said: "Apart from a quarter of an hour in the first half we coped well and I was delighted with the result." Merson limped off three minutes from time with a twisted ankle.

September 11

Ipswich veteran John Wark paused when he was asked how he rated the Arsenal strike force of Kevin Campbell and Ian Wright. He had just seen his team destroyed by a Campbell hat-trick, two of the goals made by Wright, who scored one himself first.

He could have been forgiven a brusque response. Instead he paid the Highbury pair perhaps the ultimate compliment. "The best pairing I've ever known were Ian Rush and Kenny Dalglish at Liverpool," said Wark who had a close-up view of them during his days at Anfield. "These could be as good. They have all the potential."

Wark's assessment provided an authoritative footnote to an afternoon which had seen Ipswich put through the shredder. Wark, 36, called on the experience of nearly 20 years at the top, including glory days under Bobby Robson at Ipswich and 29 Scottish caps. "I was very impressed. They are a fantastic pair," he said. "Perhaps the best in the League. Before the game there were suggestions I might be used as a sweeeper to try to plug any holes. But it's questionable whether it would have made any difference with them in this kind of form. They work unselfishly for each other, always chatting one to the other, always looking for each other."

The seek-and-destroy partnership proved particularly destructive this day thanks to their special telepathy. Wright was happy to take Campbell's service on the half-hour, slotting home his fine pass. Eight minutes later Wright produced a moment of pure magic to set up the second. David Linighan and Micky Stockwell were transfixed as Wright juggled the ball from foot to foot before lobbing it over goalkeeper Craig Forrest. The ball struck the bar and Campbell was on hand to help himself.

Paul Merson and Nigel Winterburn conspired to set up Campbell's next, a header after 55 minutes. But normal service was resumed nine minutes later when Wright gave Campbell the platform to complete his hat-trick.

ARSENAL 4

IPSWICH 0
(Half-time score: 2-0)

Arsenal: Seaman, Keown, Winterburn, Davis, Linighan, Adams, Jensen (Hillier), Wright, Campbell, Merson (Limpar), McGoldrick.
Sub: Miller.
Ipswich: Forrest, Stockwell, Wark, Linighan, Thompson, Whelan, Palmer, Williams, Whitton, Kiwomya, Goddard.
Subs: Yallop, Guentchev, Baker.
Scorers: Arsenal: Wright 30, Campbell 38, 55, 64.
Referee: J Worrall (Warrington)
Attendance: 28,563

League Table After Match

	P	W	D	L	F	A	Pts
Man Utd.	7	5	1	1	14	4	16
Arsenal	7	5	1	1	11	5	16
Blackburn	7	4	2	1	10	6	14
Coventry	7	3	4	0	11	6	13
Liverpool	7	4	0	3	13	5	12
Aston Villa	7	3	3	1	9	5	12
Wimbledon	7	3	3	1	9	6	12
Everton	7	4	0	3	8	6	12
Norwich	7	3	2	2	11	8	11
Tottenham	7	3	2	2	7	6	11
Ipswich	7	3	2	2	7	7	11
Leeds	7	3	1	3	6	9	10
Chelsea	7	2	3	2	7	6	9
QPR	7	3	0	4	10	14	9
Man City	7	2	2	3	8	7	8
Sheffield Utd.	7	2	2	3	11	14	8
Newcastle	6	1	3	2	5	6	6
Oldham	7	1	2	4	5	10	5
West Ham	7	1	2	4	3	11	5
Southampton	7	1	0	6	7	12	3
Sheffield Wed	6	0	3	3	4	9	3
Swindon	7	0	2	5	3	17	2

September 15

ODENSE 1

ARSENAL 2
(Half-time score: 1-1)

Odense: Hogh, Nedergaard, Hemmingsen, Steen-Nielsen, Helveg, Nielsen, Sangild, Dethlefsen, Thorup, Tchami, Skaarup.
Subs: Hjorth, Damsted, Brogger, Petterson, Sterob.
Arsenal: Seaman, Selley, Winterburn, Davis, Linighan, Keown, Jensen, Wright (Smith), Campbell, Merson, McGoldrick.
Subs: Bould, Hillier, Parlour, Miller.
Bookings: Arsenal: Jensen (foul), Campbell (foul).
Scorers: Odense: Keown (o.g.) 18; Arsenal: Wright 35, Merson 68.
Referee: A Cakar (Turkey)
Attendance: 9,580

FIRST ROUND, FIRST LEG

The birthplace of Hans Christian Andersen would seem to be the perfect place for a fairy-tale start, and that was just what Ian Wright made to his European adventure. The England striker, determined to prove himself in Europe, gave Arsenal the equaliser they desperately needed after Odense had taken the lead in a tense first-round, first-leg Cup Winners' Cup tie.

Then Paul Merson, with a stunning second goal which temporarily eased the worries over his future at Highbury, gave them an invaluable cushion of two away goals to take to the home leg.

Wright's pace and uncanny instinct for an opening might have brought early reward but it was the Danes who could have taken the lead after only three minutes.

Odense won a debatable penalty when the lanky striker Jess Thorup charged into the area and went sprawling after a challenge from Andy Linighan. Thorup picked himself up, placed the ball on the spot and hit it the wrong side of a post.

Arsenal were not so lucky in the 18th minute when Odense took the lead. Brian Skaarup and Brian Steen-Nielsen juggled the ball between them after a corner before Skaarup's speculative cross struck Martin Keown's leg and flew past the startled David Seaman.

Wright replied after 35 minutes. John Jensen fed Paul Davis and his inspired pass spun away from goalkeeper Lars Hogh. Wright, following up, had the simplest of tasks putting the ball into the net.

Wright nearly gave Arsenal a 51st-minute lead after Kevin Campbell headed the ball into his path. But the Gunners were fortunate a minute later when Eddie McGoldrick headed across his own goal and the Cameroon striker Alphonse Tchami's shot brought a superb save from Seaman.

Campbell added to his growing reputation and Merson confirmed his individual flair when they combined for Arsenal's 68th-minute winner. Merson raced on to Campbell's pass and left two defenders flat-footed before slotting home a goal to cherish.

Campbell – booked along with Jensen by an over-zealous referee – might have added a third in the 77th-minute but he hit his shot wide when well placed.

September 19

There were 44,000 inside Old Trafford and Gary Pallister spoke for every one of them when he marvelled at the pace and power of Eric Cantona's match-winning goal. "It was like an Exocet," he said. "Eric is known for his guile, his caressing of the ball. Then, when the feeling is right, he just goes in and hits it. As soon as that shot left his foot you knew it was in the net."

But if the explosives came from Cantona, the heroics came from Steve Bruce who suffered a head wound in a 21st-minute clash with Kevin Campbell and played on swathed in a bandage. "He needed five stitches," said manager Alex Ferguson, "three in the first half and two at the interval when his brain started to seep through."

The match grew to a panting crescendo with John Jensen and Paul Ince snapping and snarling in midfield. Yet in the first half Peter Schmeichel could have leaned against his post while surveying the distant action.

David Seaman soon realised his 30th birthday would be no party and was grateful when Mark Hughes directed a header narrowly wide. Then, in the 37th minute, came Cantona. David Hillier obstructed Ince 30 yards from goal. Free-kick. A touch by Ince and a detonation by Cantona's right boot. No bullet could have been fired more effectively.

Ince should have sewn the game up more tidily in the 52nd minute but his finish was disappointing after an astute pass from Roy Keane. By now Arsenal were forcing their way into a contest which had seemed beyond them. Half-chances fell their way, the best to Campbell who was foiled by Denis Irwin's outstretched foot.

Ian Wright, suffering limited service, brought Schmeichel speedily off his line and the Danish goalkeeper had to save again as Campbell went for the rebound. As the action intensified, so did the passion. Keane and Martin Keown had already earned cautions from referee Vic Callow before an ugly spat erupted between Hughes and Paul Davis. Hughes ran 20 yards to flatten the Arsenal midfielder after being caught by a late challenge. He was lucky to escape with only a yellow card.

MANCHESTER UNITED 1

ARSENAL 0
(Half-time score: 1-0)

Man Utd: Schmeichel, Parker, Irwin, Bruce, Sharpe, Pallister, Cantona, Ince, Keane, Hughes, Giggs.
Subs: McClair, Kanchelskis, Sealey.
Arsenal: Seaman, Keown, Winterburn, Linighan, Adams, Hillier (Davis), Jensen, Wright, Campbell, Merson (Smith), McGoldrick.
Sub: Miller.
Bookings: Man Utd: Keane (foul), Hughes (foul); Arsenal: Keown (ungentlemanly conduct).
Scorer: Man Utd: Cantona 38.
Referee: V Callow (Solihull)
Attendance: 44,009

League Table After Match

	P	W	D	L	F	A	Pts
Man Utd.	8	6	1	1	15	4	19
Arsenal	8	5	1	2	11	6	16
Aston Villa	8	4	3	1	11	6	15
Everton	8	5	0	3	10	6	15
Tottenham	8	4	2	2	12	6	14
Coventry	8	3	5	0	12	7	14
Blackburn	8	4	2	2	10	8	14
Leeds	8	4	1	3	8	10	13
Liverpool	8	4	0	4	13	7	12
Norwich	8	3	3	2	13	10	12
Wimbledon	7	3	3	1	9	6	12
Ipswich	8	3	2	3	8	9	11
Newcastle	8	2	4	2	11	10	10
Chelsea	8	2	4	2	8	7	10
QPR	8	3	1	4	12	16	10
Man City	7	2	2	3	8	7	8
Sheffield Utd	8	2	2	4	12	16	8
West Ham	8	2	2	4	5	11	8
Sheffield Wed	8	1	3	4	8	13	6
Oldham	8	1	2	5	5	15	5
Southampton	8	1	0	7	7	14	3
Swindon	8	0	3	5	5	19	3

September 21

HUDDERSFIELD 0

ARSENAL 5
(Half-time score: 0-2)

Huddersfield: Francis, Trevitt, Billy, Starbuck, Hicks, Dyson, Dunn, Robinson, Booth, Marsden, Wells.
Subs: Collins, Onvara, Blackwell.
Arsenal: Seaman, Keown, Winterburn, Davis , Linighan, Adams, Jensen (Hillier), Wright, Campbell, Merson (Smith), McGoldrick.
Sub: Miller.
Scorers: Arsenal: Wright 6, 63, 82, Campbell 15, Merson 57.
Referee: J Lloyd (Wrexham)
Attendance: 14,275

George Graham had feared that his side's exertions against Odense and Manchester United in the previous seven days might affect their efforts in their opening Coca-Cola Cup tie. He could not have been more wrong.

In their third outing in a week Arsenal forgot all about their leaden legs to annihilate Neil Warnock's Second Division strugglers. Warnock had described Arsenal as the most difficult team in the country to beat and Graham as the best manager in the business. He could only watch in admiration as those words were endorsed.

Under dripping skies Ian Wright mopped up a brilliant hat-trick and there were other goals for Kevin Campbell and Paul Merson as the Yorkshire club were engulfed by a tide of attacking football. Wright took less than six minutes to put Arsenal in front, nipping through to convert a pass from Eddie McGoldrick. Surprisingly, perhaps, it was his first goal in seven meetings with Huddersfield.

Then Wright turned provider after being up-ended in the 14th-minute. From the free-kick he swapped passes for Campbell to squeeze in the second. Merson hit the bar five minutes before the break but made amends on the hour, forcing the ball home after Campbell's first effort had been saved by Steve Francis.

The best was still to come and Wright provided it in the 63rd minute. Spotting goalkeeper Francis fractionally off his line, Wright took aim from 20 yards to leave Francis stranded and desperately flapping as the ball sailed over him and into the net.

Wright concluded his imperious night's work by converting Tony Adams's pass for his third eight minutes from the end.

"I had wondered if three matches in a week would tire my side but they answered that with a terrific exhibition of quality passing and finishing," said Graham. "We always treat the opposition with respect and our attitude tonight was tremendous."

The only controversial note on a night of triumph was struck by Merson, who flung down a tie-up when he was substituted 12 minutes from the end and strode straight to the dressing room without looking at the Arsenal bench.

Graham denied he was at odds with his player. "There was no discord," he said. "It was a straightforward decision."

September 25

George Graham watched Paul Merson maintain his own run for glory with the winning goal and then had words of sympathy for the man it had hurt most.

Southampton manager Ian Branfoot, the target of a vitriolic campaign to unseat him at The Dell, had come in for more abuse at the end of the match. It was a sustained attack which would eventually see him resign. "I feel for him," said Graham. "I find what is happening distasteful. He is a good manager at a good club."

Graham and Branfoot, who chatted over a cup of tea after the match, could find common ground in their handling of certain stars: Arsenal's Merson and Southampton's Matthew Le Tissier. Both managers, frustrated by lack of application from these talented players, had dropped them in recent matches. But, while Le Tissier was again missing from the team which travelled to Highbury, Merson was bringing a smile to Graham's face with a fine comeback performance plus the winning goal.

A Kevin Campbell cross was punched out by goalkeeper Tim Flowers. Jeff Kenna was challenged by Eddie McGoldrick and the ball dropped for Merson to add the finishing touch with a spectacular overhead kick in the third minute of first-half injury time.

If that was bad timing for Southampton, they suffered bad fortune in the second half when young Paul Moody, given the simplest of chances in front of goal, lobbed the ball over the bar. "He would have put it away without thinking in training," said Branfoot. "But he cost just £15,000 from Waterlooville...and he was playing at Highbury."

ARSENAL 1
SOUTHAMPTON 0
(Half-time score: 1-0)

Arsenal: Seaman, Keown, Winterburn, Davis (Hillier), Linighan, Adams, Jensen, Wright, Campbell, Merson, McGoldrick.
Subs: Limpar, Miller.
Southampton: Flowers, Kenna, Moore, Wood, Moody, Cockerill, Maddison, Allen, Adams, Dowie, Monkou.
Subs: Benali, Banger, Andrews.
Booking: Southampton: Benali (foul).
Scorer: Arsenal: Merson 45.
Referee: K Morton (Bury St. Edmunds)
Attendance: 26,902

Hit and kiss: Wright congratulates Merson

League Table After Match

	P	W	D	L	F	A	Pts
Man Utd.	9	7	1	1	19	6	22
Arsenal.............	9	6	1	2	12	6	19
Aston Villa	9	4	4	1	12	7	16
Leeds.	9	5	1	3	10	10	16
Norwich............	9	4	3	2	18	11	15
Tottenham	9	4	3	2	14	8	15
Wimbledon	8	4	3	1	10	6	15
Blackburn	9	4	3	2	11	9	15
Everton	9	5	0	4	11	11	15
Coventry...........	9	3	5	1	12	9	14
Newcastle..........	9	3	4	2	13	10	13
Chelsea..............	9	3	4	2	9	7	13
Liverpool	9	4	0	5	13	8	12
Ipswich.............	9	3	3	3	10	11	12
Man City...........	9	3	2	4	9	8	11
QPR	8	3	1	4	12	16	10
Sheffield Utd.....	9	2	2	5	12	17	8
West Ham..........	9	2	2	5	5	13	8
Sheffield Wed ..	9	1	4	4	9	14	7
Oldham.............	9	1	3	5	6	16	6
Southampton	9	1	0	8	7	15	3
Swindon	9	0	3	6	7	23	3

September 29

ARSENAL 1

ODENSE 1
(Half-time score: 0-0)
(Arsenal won 3-2 on aggregate)

Arsenal: Seaman, Dixon, Winterburn, Davis, Keown, Adams, Jensen, Wright (Smith), Campbell, Merson, McGoldrick.
Subs: Linighan, Miller, Selley, Limpar.
Odense: Hogh, Nedergaard, Hemmingsen, Steen-Nielsen, Helveg, Nielsen, Hjorth, Dethlefsen, Thorup, Tchami, Skaarup.
Subs: Melvang, Damsted, Brogger, Petersen, Sterobo.
Bookings: Arsenal: Keown (foul); Odense: Neilsen (foul), Skaarup (foul).
Scorers: Arsenal: Campbell 52; Odense: Nielsen 86.
Referee: H J Weber (Germany)
Attendance: 25,689

FIRST ROUND, SECOND LEG

Kevin Campbell conjured up dreams of European glory for Arsenal which were then almost shattered in a nightmarish ending at Highbury.

After Campbell's strike Arsenal were going through the motions until rudely awakened from their sleep-walking by a goal four minutes from time by Odense's former Bayern Munich star Allan Nielsen.

Arsenal's relief at hearing the final whistle was obvious. In those final moments several players and thousands of fans had relived the horror of the European Cup defeat by Benfica two seasons earlier. Then, another Campbell goal in the first leg had offered the prospect of a famous scalp until the Portuguese champions struck back in the return leg and clinched victory in injury time. Luckily Odense, for all their organisation and effort, were no Benfica.

Arsenal had put caution before invention despite their 2-1 first-leg victory and their no-risk policy looked able to answer any questions the Danes might ask.

Andy Linighan, Arsenal's FA Cup hero four months earlier, was demoted to the bench to leave space for the return of Lee Dixon in his first appearance since damaging a foot on the opening day of the season and Martin Keown was given a marking job on Alphonse Tchami who had scored four goals for Odense in domestic action the previous weekend.

It was 13 minutes before the visitors' goal was threatened and then Paul Merson crashed the ball against a wall of bodies. Odense briefly showed their attacking flair when Jess Thorup, who had missed a penalty in the first leg, saw a glancing header from a Nielsen cross flash wide.

On the half-hour Tony Adams, who had missed the first leg through suspension following two bookings in the previous European campaign, should have marked his re-appearance in Europe in dramatic fashion with the opening goal.

Paul Davis looped the ball over an Odense defence appealing for offside and Adams, who had been doubtful until shortly before the

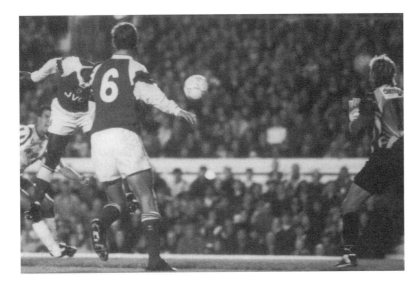

Campbell's super: Campbell jumps to head Arsenal's goal

kick-off with an ankle injury, hurried his volley and hit it over the bar. Then, just before half-time, he went close with a header.

Campbell seemed to have negotiated a safe if unspectacular route through to the second round with his 52nd-minute goal, rising to power home a far-post header from a Davis free-kick.

Keown was booked for keeping too close an eye on Tchami and Odense's Brian Nielsen and Brian Skaarup were also cautioned as the second half threatened to peter out in petty scuffling.

Then Allan Nielsen struck to set the alarm bells ringing. His first shot spun off Dixon and, while Arsenal's defenders momentarily froze, he hammered in the rebound. The remaining time was spent in a frenzy of action before Hans Weber of Germany blew his whistle and Arsenal let out a collective sigh of relief.

October 2

LIVERPOOL 0

ARSENAL 0

Liverpool: Grobbelaar, Jones, Dicks, Wright, Hutchison, Clough, Stewart, Rush, Redknapp, Fowler, Ruddock.
Subs: Whelan, McManaman, James.
Arsenal: Seaman, Dixon, Winterburn, Davis, Linighan, Adams, Jensen, Wright, Campbell, Merson, McGoldrick.
Subs: Smith, Parlour, Miller.
Bookings: Liverpool: Stewart (dissent); Arsenal: Wright (ungentlemanly conduct).
Referee: G Ashby (Worcs)
Attendance: 42,750

There was no official ceremony but the 42,750 crowd at Anfield knew they had witnessed a significant moment in English soccer. They had seen the transfer of an international shirt from one player to the other.

Lee Dixon, England right-back for most of Graham Taylor's tenure, was put up for comparison with 21-year-old Rob Jones who had lost almost all of the previous season through injury. The signs were that Jones had rehabilitated well and his continued good form throughout the remainder of the season caused Terry Venables to select him, but not Dixon, in his opening England squad for the match with Denmark on March 9.

In truth, apart from this absorbing comparison, there was little to recommend a match that celebrated Liverpool's 500th minute without a Premiership goal. Arsenal themselves rarely looked like scoring and their assistant manager Stewart Houston admitted: "We were a bit below par and Liverpool looked sharper than us."

That Arsenal kept a clean sheet was thanks to England goalkeeper David Seaman, who reaffirmed his No 1 status with an excellent display of shot-stopping, including one outstanding effort that denied Robbie Fowler his debut goal.

League Table After Match

	P	W	D	L	F	A	Pts
Man Utd.	10	8	1	1	22	8	25
Arsenal	10	6	2	2	12	7	20
Leeds.	10	6	1	3	14	10	19
Norwich	10	5	3	2	19	11	18
Blackburn	10	5	3	2	14	10	18
Newcastle	10	4	4	2	15	10	16
Aston Villa	10	4	4	2	12	9	16
Wimbledon	10	4	4	2	11	11	16
Tottenham	9	4	3	2	14	8	15
Everton	9	5	0	4	11	11	15
Coventry	10	3	5	2	12	10	14
QPR	10	4	2	4	16	17	14
Liverpool	10	4	1	5	13	8	13
Chelsea	10	3	4	3	9	8	13
Ipswich	10	3	3	4	10	14	12
Man City	9	3	2	4	9	8	11
West Ham	10	3	2	5	6	13	11
Sheffield Utd.	10	2	3	5	15	20	9
Sheffield Wed	10	1	4	5	11	17	7
Oldham	9	1	3	5	6	16	6
Southampton	10	1	1	8	10	18	4
Swindon	10	0	3	7	8	26	3

October 5

SECOND ROUND, SECOND LEG

Huddersfield came to Highbury to rediscover their pride and found it. Arsenal were left with a video nasty which George Graham insisted they watched the following day at the training ground. "Why should I be the only one to suffer," he complained. "They'll be back in tomorrow just to watch the recording."

What the players would have seen was a lacklustre, lackadaisical display as too many players simply went through the motions in the clear belief that the tie had been decided in the first leg.

The fans who jeered the players off at the end had Graham's sympathy. "They are entitled to react," he said. "I was very disappointed. I would have liked to have played more youngsters but then I would have been accused of fielding a weakened team.

"As it was we played weakly. We treated the game too lightly and the players know how I feel."

Huddersfield made it a miserable return to action for Steve Bould, playing only his third senior game since an operation on his damaged thigh the previous January. He miscued a back-pass to goalkeeper David Seaman and Ian Dunn, a recruit from non-League Goole Town, nipped through to slide the ball home.

Arsenal took the edge off their embarrassment with a 63rd-minute equaliser. Alan Smith climaxed his first full game of the season by firing home Eddie McGoldrick's fine run and cross.

Huddersfield manager Neil Warnock said: "At half-time and one up I told the lads to lock up and get on the bus. Some people came here to see a double-figure job but we were playing for our pride. I'm just glad it wasn't a farce."

No farce, perhaps, but for Arsenal it was no laughing matter either.

ARSENAL 1

HUDDERSFIELD 1
(Half-time score: 0-1)
(Arsenal won 6-1 on aggregate)

Arsenal: Seaman, Dixon, Winterburn, Parlour, Linighan, Bould, Jensen (Selley), Smith, Campbell, Limpar, McGoldrick (Heaney).
Sub: Miller.
Huddersfield: Francis, Trevitt, Billy, Starbuck, Hicks, Jackson, Dunn, Robinson, Booth, Dyson, Wells.
Subs: Roberts, Onvara, Blackwell.
Scorers: Arsenal: Smith 63; Huddersfield: Dunn 44.
Referee: K Cooper (Pontypridd)
Attendance: 18,789

Call to arms: Arsenal's scorer Alan Smith tussles with the Huddersfield defence

October 16

ARSENAL 0

MANCHESTER CITY 0

Arsenal: Seaman, Dixon, Winterburn, Davis, Linighan, Adams, Heaney (Campbell), Wright, Smith, Parlour, McGoldrick
Subs: Keown, Will.
Man City: Coton, Edghill, Kernaghan, Curle, Phelan, Flitcroft, McMahon, Simpson, Lomas, Sheron, Quinn.
Subs: Mike, D Brightwell, Dibble.
Booking: Man City: Coton (handling outside area).
Referee: R Milford (Bristol)
Attendance: 44,009

Standard Liege sent their spies to watch Arsenal in preparation for the following Wednesday's second round of the European Cup Winners' Cup. They reportedly left claiming they had nothing to fear. Little were they to know.

But their false sense of security was understandable on the evidence of this dismal game.

George Graham again shuffled his pack. Paul Merson, who had been considered good enough by Graham Taylor to oust club colleague Ian Wright from the England team against Holland, did not even make the bench. And Kevin Campbell came on as substitute when it was too late to redeem a lacklustre draw. Tony Adams and Ray Parlour, in the news for an off-the-field incident involving a pizza parlour and a fire extinguisher, were the subjects of numerous wisecracks from the crowd. And David Seaman endured an afternoon of City fans chanting "Where were you when Koeman scored?"

Graham later explained his decision to axe Merson as well as John Jensen and Anders Limpar, also back from international duty. "Hopefully we'll play 60 games this season and I have to balance the team. The league is a nine-month race but two errors in Europe and you are out. I view Wednesday's game against Liege as far more important than today's. I've spoken to Merson and he fully understands the need to be rested after playing for England. It was a good chance to blood some youngsters."

City edged a soporific first half with Arsenal old boy Niall Quinn going close with an early volley and Richard Edghill sending a left-foot shot screaming inches high.

Arsenal showed more passion after the break with Paul Davis volleying just over and Eddie McGoldrick testing Tony Coton with a fierce, low drive.

But the main talking point came when Keith Curle's header inadvertently hit the advancing Coton's hands outside the City area. Referee Roger Milford, presumably deciding the goalkeeper's actions had not been deliberate which would have warranted a sending off, settled the issue with a yellow card for Coton and a free-kick for Arsenal which Nigel Winterburn blasted high into the new

North Bank stand.

City manager Brian Horton, beaten only once in his first eight games in charge, revealed: "George told me he wouldn't want a sending-off for such an offence and I agree."

League Table After Match

	P	W	D	L	F	A	Pts
Man Utd.	11	9	1	1	24	9	28
Norwich	11	6	3	2	21	12	21
Arsenal	11	6	3	2	12	6	21
Leeds.	11	6	2	3	14	10	20
Blackburn	11	5	4	2	14	10	19
Tottenham	11	5	3	3	18	12	18
Aston Villa	11	4	5	2	12	9	17
QPR	11	5	2	4	18	18	17
Wimbledon	11	4	5	2	13	13	17
Liverpool	11	5	1	5	15	9	16
Newcastle	11	4	4	3	16	12	16
Everton	11	5	1	5	14	15	16
Coventry	11	3	6	2	13	11	15
Man City	11	3	4	4	10	9	13
Chelsea	11	3	4	4	10	10	13
Ipswich	11	3	4	4	10	14	13
West Ham	11	3	3	5	6	13	12
Sheffield Utd.	11	2	4	5	15	20	10
Sheffield Wed	11	1	5	5	13	19	8
Oldham	11	1	4	6	8	19	7
Southampton	11	1	2	8	11	19	5
Swindon	11	0	4	7	9	27	4

October 20

ARSENAL 3

STANDARD LIEGE 0
(Half-time score: 1-0)

Arsenal: Seaman, Dixon, Winterburn, Davis, Keown (Linighan), Adams, Jensen, Wright (Campbell), Smith, Merson, McGoldrick.
Subs: Miller, Limpar, Parlour.
Standard Liege: Munaron, Genaux, Leonard, Rednic, Lashas, Pister, Hellers, Vervoort, Asselman, Van Rooy, Wilmots.
Subs: Goossens, Niyens, Bisconti, Soudan, Smeets.
Bookings: Arsenal: Wright (foul); Liege: Vervoort (foul), Rednic (foul).
Scorers: Arsenal: Wright 39, 64, Merson 51.
Referee: F Kaupe (Austria)
Attendance: 25,258

SECOND ROUND, FIRST LEG

Ian Wright, desperately disappointed by England's World Cup failure in Holland seven days earlier, took his revenge on the Belgians of Standard Liege with two superb goals.

He was also pole-axed twice by Liege defenders in off-the-ball incidents and collected a booking. It was, as he agreed afterwards, an eventful night. "I'm just glad my nose wasn't broken," he said. "But George Graham has taught me to count to ten...and punish the opposition by scoring. Don't get mad, get even is my philosophy. Vengeance is the inspiration."

Liege, despite five defeats in 11 League games, arrived with a reputation for uncompromising defence. That was soon in evidence.

When Wright was felled for the first time after nine minutes the game could have turned ugly. The Arsenal bench were clearly under the impression that an elbow from Thierry Pister had been responsible and Gunners' coach Stewart Houston was involved in a heated exchange with the Liege dug-out. It had occurred as Lee Dixon prepared to take a free-kick and Austrian referee Friedrich Kaupe was unsighted.

"I was caught on the side of the face," said Wright. "Retaliation doesn't give me as much pleasure as running past them after scoring."

That pleasure was to come after referee Kaupe had spotted Eddie McGoldrick being up-ended for the third time in succession and booked Liege's Patrick Vervoort. As Arsenal pressed forward for only their fourth goal in 360 minutes of Highbury action, Martin Keown provided the vital cross from the right six minutes before half-time. Wright, with typical anticipation and pace, darted in front of the Liege defence to head home. Arsenal's confidence soared.

Merson added a superb second in the 51st minute direct from a free-kick which should have brought a sending-off for Mircea Rednic. He deliberately handled the ball to prevent a clear goalscoring chance for Wright but, shades of England's debacle in Rotterdam, he was only cautioned like Holland's Ronald Koeman had been for his foul on David Platt. This time, though, Merson made them pay in the most emphatic fashion.

Wright powers home his second goal

"It was a definite red card," said Graham. "I only hope we get the same leniency when we play away."

Wright had his consolation in the 54th minute, chipping his second over the goalkeeper after a superbly timed run. "Not many strikers could have got that goal," said Merson. "His finish was second to none."

Graham was delighted with the performance. "We outpassed the Continentals," he said. "We denied them time and space, then played some outstanding football. If you sit back against sides like these they can hurt you, but we imposed ourselves on them." And none more than Wright.

October 23

OLDHAM 0
ARSENAL 0

Oldham: Gerrard, Fleming, Makin, Redmond, Halle, Brennan, Milligan, Bernard, Sharp, Beckford, Holden.
Subs: Beresford, Barlow, Key.
Arsenal: Seaman, Dixon, Winterburn, Davis, Linighan, Adams, Hillier (Campbell), Wright, Smith, Merson, McGoldrick.
Subs: Bould, Miller.
Sent off: Oldham: Holden (violent conduct).
Booking: Arsenal: Dixon (dissent).
Referee: M Reed (Birmingham)
Attendance: 12,105

Referee Mike Reed showed a red card to Oldham and a green light to Arsenal's need to stiffen their presence in the title chase. Oldham winger Rick Holden went at red for a push on Lee Dixon that seemed worthy of no more than a caution but Arsenal stopped at green – inexplicably, tamely and, as it was to prove, irrecoverably.

George Graham said he was happy enough with the pressure applied to Oldham's 10 men for 53 minutes and regretted only the lack of "clinical finishing". He said that publicly. What he said privately was no doubt a different matter. The substance of it would be regret at his team's failure to seize the mantle of legitimate title challengers.

Joe Royle's Oldham played with their usual heart and impressive feel for real football, yet they would surely have been put to the sword by a team who believed in their destiny. Arsenal, though, never rose above metronomic efficiency. Paul Merson looked the best player on the field and Tony Adams provided his usual heart-on-sleeve commitment. But no one could lay claim to the three points.

Ian Wright, mostly contained with brilliant economy of effort by stand-in central defender Craig Fleming, Kevin Campbell, a second-half substitute for David Hillier, and Alan Smith all had shots well saved by Paul Gerrard, and Adams snatched at one perfect opportunity.

But this was no relentless tide of aggression. In fact, Oldham might have sneaked a win on the stroke of time when Dixon appeared to handle in the box. Graham blamed the midweek European action for the less than sparkling performamce. But this third goalless Premiership match in a row suggested that Arsenal would have to look elsewhere for honours this season.

Safety first: Lee Dixon is given
a police escort off the Boundary
Park pitch after his bust-up
with Rick Holden

League Table After Match

	P	W	D	L	F	A	Pts
Man Utd.	12	10	1	1	25	9	31
Norwich	12	6	4	2	21	12	22
Arsenal	12	6	4	2	12	6	22
Leeds	12	6	3	3	17	13	21
QPR	12	6	2	4	23	19	20
Blackburn	12	5	5	2	17	13	20
Aston Villa	12	5	5	2	13	9	20
Tottenham	12	5	4	3	19	13	19
Liverpool	12	5	2	5	16	10	17
Wimbledon	11	4	5	2	13	13	17
Newcastle	12	4	4	4	17	14	16
Everton	12	5	1	6	14	16	16
Coventry	12	3	6	3	14	16	15
Man City	12	3	5	4	11	10	14
Chelsea	12	3	4	5	10	11	13
Ipswich	11	3	4	4	10	14	13
West Ham	12	3	4	5	6	13	13
Sheffield Utd.	12	2	5	5	16	21	11
Sheffield Wed	12	1	6	5	14	20	9
Southampton	12	2	2	8	13	20	8
Oldham	12	1	5	6	8	19	8
Swindon	12	0	5	7	10	28	5

October 26

ARSENAL 1

NORWICH 1
(Half-time score: 0-1)

Arsenal: Seaman, Dixon, Winterburn, Linighan, Adams, McGoldrick (Davis), Jensen, Parlour, Merson (Campbell), Wright, Smith.
Sub: Miller.
Norwich: Gunn, Culverhouse, Prior, Butterworth, Bowen, Newman, Crook, Goss, Fox, Eadie, Sutton.
Subs: Megson, Sutch, Howie.
Booking: Arsenal: Adams (foul).
Scorers: Arsenal: Wright 78; Norwich: Crook 33.
Referee: A Gunn (Sussex)
Attendance: 24,519

THIRD ROUND

Just when it seemed the Gunners had run out of bullets, up popped that man Ian Wright again with his own brand of ammunition. The boos were starting to echo around Highbury as testament to a night of frustration when Wright restored their remarkable cup run with a ferocious volley 12 minutes from time.

Arsenal thus stretched their unbeaten sequence in the Cups – FA, League and European Cup Winners' – to 23 games, but their reliance on Wright was all too evident. In that run Wright had scored 22 times. Of the meagre 24 goals Arsenal had scored all season up to this game, Wright had claimed 13.

A replay at Carrow Road was a slightly flattering reward for Arsenal on this form. Norwich had proved their new-found right to compete with the best in Europe with a brand of quality football: quick, simple passes played with the minimum of fuss. The fulcrum was Ian Crook, a player discarded by Spurs but who, in this match, ran the midfield with range and intelligence.

It was the kind of playmaking Arsenal lacked, especially as they had rested Paul Davis in favour of the ball-winning Ray Parlour.

When Arsenal did get the ball behind the Norwich defence they looked dangerous. But, as their frustration built, so they abandoned what degree of method they had shown and began to hit channel balls.

Norwich used Ian Culverhouse as sweeper and looked comfortably able to restrict Arsenal to long-range shooting. Meanwhile Chris Sutton was giving Tony Adams a torrid time to underline his potential.

Sutton slipped past Adams on the edge of the penalty area in the first half to force Seaman into a full-length save. And Sutton was instrumental in Norwich taking the lead when he sent Ruel Fox scampering down the right in the 33rd minute. Fox went round Nigel Winterburn and, when John Jensen failed to clear the cross, Crook volleyed home.

Jensen had earlier had a shot cleared off the line as Arsenal threatened a breakthrough. Paul Merson's cross was flicked on by Eddie McGoldrick and Jensen drove the ball goalwards where Culverhouse was perfectly placed to intercept.

It looked even more serious for Arsenal when Rob Newman released Sutton and Adams brought him down on the edge of the area. There were fears he could be given the red card; instead referee Allan Gunn reached for yellow and the let-off was completed as Sutton's kick thudded into the Arsenal wall.

Lee Dixon wasted a good second-half chance, shooting wide with an unimpaired sight at goal. Arsenal were looking disjointed and Wright was lectured by Mr Gunn for a heated exchange with a linesman.

As Arsenal's passes became longer and more aimless, so the anxiety of the home crowd surfaced with a spate of booing. It came as relief all round when a ball from Alan Smith bounced once and sat up perfectly for Wright to volley powerfully into the net.

George Graham insisted he had not been too disappointed. "They are the best away team in the country," he said, "and we don't mind going there for the replay."

October 30

ARSENAL 0

NORWICH 0

Arsenal: Seaman, Dixon, Winterburn (Keown), Davis, Bould, Adams, Jensen, Wright, Smith (Campbell), Merson, Limpar.
Sub: Miller.
Norwich : Gunn. Culverhouse, Newman, Butterworth, Bowen, Megson, Crook, Eadie, Fox, Prior, Sutton.
Subs: Johnson, Akinibiyi, Howie.
Bookings: Arsenal: Winterburn (foul), Bould (foul); Norwich: Sutton (foul).
Referee: R Dilkes (Mossley)
Attendance: 30,516

The groans that greeted the news that Manchester United had turned around their match against QPR to win 2-1 told the story after yet another goalless draw for Arsenal.

But quite how Norwich survived the Arsenal assault of the last 20 minutes is a matter of debate. Who said Arsenal were lucky?

Out-gunned: Norwich goalkeeper Gunn foils Smith

Pre-season fun: Seaman takes a charitable shot at Peter Schmeichel.

Last Stand: Mick Quinn puts a penalty for Coventry as the Highbury terraces become history.

First Wright: Totally unmarked, Wright slots home one of the first of the season's winners. Sheffield Wednesday defenders can only stare in disbelief.

Hero turned villain: Wright takes one of the first of the season's bookings.

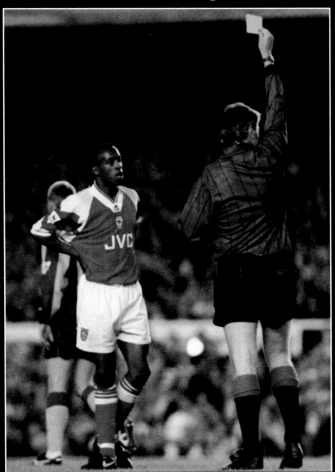

Another day, another goal: Wright and his fans salute each other.

Even Southall has no chance against the flying Ian Wright.

Ipswich defenders fall at the dancing feet of the great Arsenal striker.

A study in concentration, but Linighan causes Wright to hit the bar.

Campbell points his way to the top after burying Ipswich with his second goal of the game.

Speed and skill help the Gunners to a 1-0 victory over Southampton.

A late night out in Europe.

Head and shoulders above the rest – but not enough to score.

The Belgians tumble as Wright takes a stroll on a triumphant October evening.

Seaman goes down in agony as concerned team-mates look on.

Alan Smith heads the winner and the Geordies can do nothing.

Smith Can-Can: keeping the ball away from Newcastle.

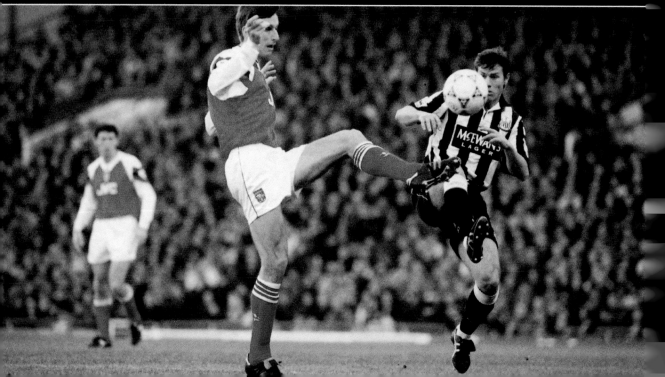

The deadly duo celebrate Swindon's downfall.

Kick Start: Ray Parlour sees in the New Year with a goal against Wimbledon.

Steve Redmond of Oldham sends Wright flying.

Giant Leap: Ian Wright at full speed narrowly misses QPR's Jan Stejskal who saves the day.

The gap between them and Manchester United grew to 11 points after this disappointing result but manager George Graham remained optimistic. "The gap doesn't worry me in the slightest," he insisted. "How many points were we behind Leeds in 1970-71 and yet we still pipped them by a point?"

The difference was that in that vintage season the Gunners won 11 and drew one of their last 13 games, as Graham well knew; he wore the No 8 shirt throughout.

The man wearing the same number in this game was Ian Wright and his unproductive spell at this stage of the season highlighted Graham's major problem. If Wright was not scoring goals, then Arsenal had few others who did. Already he had claimed more than half of the season's goal aggregate, though only five of his 13 had come in the Premiership.

None of Arsenal's meagre 12 Premiership goals from 13 games had come from the midfield, an area that passed the ball well without being punishingly creative. True, by now Arsenal had conceded only six, four fewer than any other defence. But being parsimonious without being productive was not endearing them to the Arsenal public although the return of Anders Limpar did offer variations for the fans and he contributed cleverly in midfield as well as attack.

Norwich maintained their unbeaten away record thanks to a combative steel that had been lacking the previous season when they conceded 65 league goals. "We had a milligram of luck," said Norwich manager Mike Walker with a wry smile. When Graham suggested a two-goal victory might have reflected the true difference in the afternoon there were no dissenters.

League Table After Match

	P	W	D	L	F	A	Pts
Man Utd.	13	11	1	1	27	10	34
Norwich	13	6	5	2	21	12	23
Arsenal	13	6	5	2	12	6	23
Blackburn	13	6	5	2	18	13	23
Aston Villa	13	6	5	2	15	10	23
Leeds.	13	6	4	3	20	16	22
Liverpool	13	6	2	5	20	12	20
QPR	13	6	2	5	24	21	20
Newcastle	13	5	4	4	21	14	19
Tottenham	13	5	4	4	19	14	19
Everton	13	6	1	6	16	16	19
Wimbledon	13	4	5	4	13	19	17
Coventry	13	3	7	3	14	16	16
Ipswich	13	4	4	5	12	16	16
Man City	12	3	5	4	11	10	14
Chelsea	13	3	4	6	10	12	13
West Ham	12	3	4	5	6	13	13
Sheffield Utd.	13	2	6	5	16	21	12
Oldham	13	2	5	6	9	19	11
Sheffield Wed	13	1	7	5	17	23	10
Southampton	13	2	2	9	15	24	8
Swindon	13	0	5	8	11	30	5

November 3

STANDARD LIEGE 0

ARSENAL 7
(Half-time score: 0-4)
(Arsenal won 10-0 on aggregate)

Standard Liege: Munaron, Genaux, Leonard, Soudan, Cruz, Pister, Hellers, Asselman, Goossens, Van Rooy, Wilmots.
Subs: Nuyens, Bisconti, Ernst, Smeets, Kimoni.
Arsenal: Seaman, Dixon, Winterburn, Davis, Keown (Bould), Adams, Jensen, Selley, Smith (McGoldrick), Merson, Campbell.
Subs: Miller, Hillier, Limpar.
Scorers: Arsenal: Smith 2, Selley 20, Adams 37, Campbell 41, 79, Merson 71, McGoldrick 81.
Referee: K Natri (Finland)
Attendance: 15,000

SECOND ROUND, SECOND LEG

George Graham took one of the biggest gambles of his managerial career and then saw Arsenal sweep into the quarter-finals of the Cup Winners' Cup on a tide of goals.

With a three-goal advantage from the first leg of the second-round tie, the Arsenal manager decided to leave out England striker Ian Wright. Arsenal's top scorer, who was not even given a place on the substitutes' bench, had been booked in the previous round and another yellow card would have earned him a suspension.

Graham was already looking ahead, to the possibility of Real Madrid in the next round in March, and he could not contemplate that without Wright. "It was one of the most difficult decisions I have had to make," said Graham.

In the end it hardly mattered as Arsenal amassed a 10-0 aggregate score to improve their previous best aggregate score in Europe, 7-1 against Staevnet of Denmark 30 years earlier.

Graham's decision looked good after only two minutes. Paul Merson floated a superb through-ball into the path of Alan Smith, who stroked the ball home for a 4-0 overall lead.

Merson, in sparkling form, might have had another five minutes later but, instead of shooting, he elected to cross the ball. A second did come, though, after 20 minutes when Kevin Campbell broke free down the right. Merson failed to connect with the cross, so did the Belgian goalkeeper Aeky Munaron and that left Ian Selley free to drive home his first goal for the club.

More goals were obviously on the cards and one came after 36 minutes. This time captain Tony Adams added the finishing touch to a Paul Davis corner. By the 41st minute Arsenal's travelling fans were chanting "Boring, boring Arsenal" in jest. As they did, Campbell produced the fourth goal.

John Jensen had a 20-yard drive saved brilliantly by the 35-year-old Munaron two minutes after the interval but Merson added a fifth after 71 minutes and Campbell scored his second eight minutes later. Eddie McGoldrick got in on the act with his first goal for the club as Arsenal went into seventh heaven.

Wright, 30 the day before, said: "As a goalscorer I would have loved to have been out there but I accepted George's decision without reservation. And I had great satisfaction in watching the lads put the ball in the net."

Smith after scoring the early goal

November 6

ARSENAL 1

ASTON VILLA 2
(Half-time score: 0-0)

Arsenal : Seaman, Dixon, Winterburn, Selley, Keown, Adams, Jensen, Wright, Campbell, Merson, Limpar.
Subs: Bould, McGoldrick, Miller.
Aston Villa: Bosnich, Barratt, Teale, McGrath, Small, Houghton, Daley, Townsend, Richardson, Saunders, Atkinson.
Subs: Spink, Whittingham, Ehiogu.
Bookings: Arsenal: Jensen (foul); Villa: Atkinson (foul).
Scorers: Arsenal: Wright 58; Villa: Whittingham 74, Townsend 90.
Referee: M Bodenham (Looe)
Attendance: 31,773

A smile or two would not have been out of place in the Aston Villa dressing-room after this result. Any team who had stolen three points after losing their goalkeeper and being largely outplayed had cause to celebrate.

But even Villa captain Kevin Richardson did not seem particularly gratified. "I didn't enjoy that," he complained. "We were defending so much. Had Ian Wright got one of those chances we would never have got back. I felt sorry for Arsenal. You can't dispute the fact they should have won."

It was an honest assessment. On chances Arsenal could have emulated their Cup Winners' Cup slaughter of Standard Liege three days earlier.

Spot check: Villa keeper Mark Bosnich saves Ian Wright's penalty

Apart from allowing Villa goalkeeper Mark Bosnich – later taken off with a hip injury – to save his 42nd-minute penalty, Wright was denied a further four goals to go with the one he scored in a combination of slack finishing or last-gasp defending.

Therein lay Arsenal's problem again. Besides a Kevin Campbell header, a 25-yard drive from John Jensen and a chip from Anders Limpar, the goal threat came from that one man.

Graham voiced fears that Wright's presence gave his players an inferiority complex, and that theory gained weight the more the game went on. Wright himself admitted: "I expect to score and I take it personally when I don't."

Even so, with 17 minutes left, Arsenal seemed assured of the points which would have put them joint second in the table. Regardless of Wright's misses, the way he turned Paul McGrath and crashed in his left-foot shot looked classy enough to win the game.

Limpar, grudgingly given a schoolmasterly report of "average but could do better" by Graham, looked the most skilful player on the pitch and gave Villa full-back Bryan Small a hellish afternoon.

But it was a switch by Ron Atkinson, which the Villa boss modestly described as "an inspired piece of tactical genius", which swayed the game. He dispensed with the services of Ray Houghton, pushed Dalian Atkinson wide and introduced substitute Guy Whittingham up front. Genius or not, the move changed the game as Whittingham broke clear to hit the equaliser.

Arsenal's problem midfield was responsible for the winner as Andy Townsend was allowed to come through and score in injury time.

"I don't want anyone to feel sorry for us," said Graham. "I just want that lucky Arsenal tag back as soon as possible."

League Table After Match

	P	W	D	L	F	A	Pts
Man Utd.	14	12	1	1	30	13	37
Norwich	14	7	5	2	23	13	26
Aston Villa	14	7	5	2	17	10	26
Leeds.	14	7	4	3	24	17	25
Liverpool	14	7	2	5	22	12	23
Arsenal	14	6	5	3	13	8	23
QPR	14	7	2	5	25	21	23
Blackburn	14	6	5	3	18	14	23
Newcastle	14	6	4	4	24	15	22
Wimbledon	14	5	5	4	16	19	20
Tottenham	14	5	4	5	19	15	19
Everton	14	6	1	7	17	18	19
Coventry	14	4	7	3	16	17	19
Ipswich	14	4	4	6	13	19	16
West Ham	14	4	4	6	9	16	16
Man City	14	3	5	6	14	16	14
Sheffield Wed	14	2	7	5	21	24	13
Chelsea	14	3	4	7	10	16	13
Sheffield Utd	14	2	6	6	17	23	12
Southampton	14	3	2	9	16	24	11
Oldham	14	2	5	7	10	22	11
Swindon	14	0	5	8	11	33	5

November 10

Norwich: Gunn, Culverhouse, Bowen, Butterworth, Polston, Newman, Eadie, Crook, Sutton, Fox, Goss.
Subs: Sutch, Megson, Howie.
Arsenal: Seaman, Dixon, Keown, Selley, Linighan, Bould, Jensen, Wright, Smith, Merson, Limpar.
Subs: Campbell, Morrow, Miller.
Scorers: Arsenal: Wright 14, 65, Merson 34.
Referee: P Foakes (Clacton)
Attendance: 16,319

THIRD ROUND REPLAY

Ian Wright pulled two more sparkling gems from his box of jewels to celebrate his 100th game for Arsenal in the only way he knows. The England striker scored twice and played a key part in the other goal as Coca-Cola Cup holders Arsenal powered their way into the fourth round.

Wright took his scoring tally to a remarkable 72 goals in his century of matches since moving across London from Crystal Palace two-and-a-half years earlier. His double made it 15 for the season and six in three Coca-Cola Cup games.

For once Norwich, the team who had climbed to such heights in Europe with their UEFA Cup defeat of Bayern Munich, had no answer. Wright had been Arsenal's saviour in the first match. This time there was no need for such a rescue mission as Arsenal moved comfortably into a home tie with Aston Villa.

Arsenal, without the injured Nigel Winterburn and virus victim Tony Adams, had already hit the bar through Alan Smith by the time they took the lead in the 14th minute.

David Seaman, who passed a late fitness test on an injured ankle, sent a deep free-kick into the Norwich box. Wright was initially foiled as goalkeeper Bryan Gunn saved at his feet. But the ball spun loose and the prolific Gunner reached it first, turned in an instant and lobbed the ball over the stranded Gunn from 18 yards for one of the goals of the season.

"It's not something you can practise," he said later. "You just try it on the night and this time it came off."

Anders Limpar, superb throughout, had a shot stopped before Seaman turned away a fierce drive from Ian Crook, whose goal had put Norwich ahead at Highbury a week earlier.

Arsenal virtually sealed their victory in the 34th minute with a goal once more set up by a long Seaman clearance. Wright's shot was blocked by the diving Gunn and Merson was there first to slot home the rebound.

It was all over in the 65th minute with another goal of glorious quality from Wright. Smith found Merson who, without looking up, curled a cross with the outside of his right foot and Wright, on the far edge of the box, pulled it down clinically and drilled it home.

November 20

Arsenal found Chelsea simple prey as they sent their London neighbours somersaulting to their sixth successive Premier League defeat of the season. Even with captain Tony Adams missing through flu, they merely adjusted a few nuts and bolts and sent the engine out purring.

"We have played excellently in our last four or five games," said George Graham. "It could have been five or six goals today."

Graham's most critical decision was to rest Anders Limpar and employ Martin Keown as a marker on Dennis Wise figuring that, if you stopped the little man, you stopped Chelsea. It worked like a dream. Without player-manager Glenn Hoddle, who was suffering from flu, Chelsea relied on the playmaking skill of Wise and Gavin Peacock. Graham simply played three centre-backs and told them to sit on this Chelsea pair.

Arsenal went about their job with customary thoroughness, so much so that they collected two yellow cards for fouls on Wise in the first 12 minutes. It took only another 15 minutes for Alan Smith to add the opening goal.

It came, almost inevitably, from a dead-ball situation. Paul Merson's corner was flicked on and eventually lashed into the net by the waiting Smith.

On the stroke of half-time it was all over. Ian Wright broke free and had a leg taken from under him by the gentlest of taps from David Lee.

It was a penalty and Wright did not miss. "He could have had a hat-trick," said Graham, "but we did more than enough."

CHELSEA 0

ARSENAL 2
(Half-time score: 0-2)

Chelsea: Kharine, Sinclair, Lee, Johnsen, Clarke, Donaghy, Barnard, Peacock, Wise, Shipperley, Stein.
Subs: Hopkin, Newton, Hitchcock.
Arsenal: Seaman, Dixon, Winterburn (Morrow), Davis, Linighan, Bould, Keown, Wright, Smith, Merson, Selley.
Subs: Campbell, Miller.
Bookings: Chelsea: Donaghy (foul); Arsenal: Keown (foul), Davis (foul).
Scorers: Arsenal: Smith 27, Wright (pen) 45.
Referee: P Don (Middlesex)
Attendance: 26,839

League Table After Match

	P	W	D	L	F	A	Pts
Man Utd.	15	13	1	1	33	13	40
Aston Villa	15	8	5	2	18	11	29
Norwich	15	7	6	2	24	14	27
QPR	15	8	2	5	28	21	26
Leeds.	15	7	5	3	25	18	26
Arsenal	15	7	5	3	15	8	26
Blackburn	15	7	5	3	20	14	26
Newcastle	15	7	4	4	27	15	25
Liverpool	15	7	2	6	22	15	23
Tottenham	15	5	5	5	20	16	20
Coventry	15	4	8	3	16	17	20
Wimbledon	15	5	5	5	17	2	20
Everton	15	6	1	8	17	21	19
West Ham	15	5	4	6	11	16	19
Ipswich	15	4	5	6	13	22	17
Man City	16	3	7	6	16	17	16
Sheffield Wed	15	2	8	5	21	24	14
Chelsea	16	3	5	8	13	18	14
Sheffield Utd.	15	2	6	7	17	24	12
Southampton	15	3	2	10	16	26	11
Oldham	15	2	5	8	10	24	11
Swindon	15	0	6	9	13	35	6

November 24

WEST HAM 0

ARSENAL 0

West Ham: Miklosko, Breacker, Burrows, Potts, Gale, Bishop, Butler, Holmes, Marsh, Morley, Chapman.
Subs: Boere, M Allen, Peyton.
Arsenal: Seaman, Dixon, Winterburn, Keown, Linighan, Bould, Morrow, Wright (Miller), Smith, Merson, Limpar (Campbell).
Sub: Davis.
Sent off: Arsenal: Seaman (foul).
Referee: P Durkin (Portland)
Attendance: 20,279

David Seaman was sent off for a professional foul but at least George Graham got back what he wanted most: Arsenal's lucky tag.

Seaman, under fire all night from West Ham's attack, came sprinting out of his area with six minutes left as Trevor Morley charged towards goal. Knowing his 15th clean sheet of the season was in jeopardy, Seaman body-checked the striker with the force of a gridiron line-backer.

Referee Paul Durkin did not hestitate to show Seaman the red card. "No complaints," said Gunners' boss Graham. "We thought Morley was offside and if that was the case the incident would not have arisen. But it was not given and David brought down the man.

Hammer blow: Seaman was sent off for this clash with Morley

The referee had a good game. I just think the linesman made a mistake."

Arsenal had good reason to remember the man with the red-trimmed flag, Paul Vosper. Two years earlier he had become the only referee to send off David O'Leary in his 20-year Highbury career.

With Seaman off the field, Arsenal had the escape that put the smile on Graham's face. Substitute goalkeeper Alan Miller came on in place of Ian Wright but looked beaten by David Burrows's drive from Matt Holmes's free-kick and it needed a goal-line clearance from Nigel Winterburn to maintain Arsenal's defensive record.

This clean sheet meant they had not conceded an away goal in more than nine weeks, although West Ham were certainly left wondering just how they had managed it. Two weeks earlier Graham had complained that people were beginning to feel sorry for his side and he wanted them to be known as lucky Arsenal again. They were that all right, with only sheer fortune keeping out Morley and Co.

"It was typical Arsenal," agreed West Ham manager Billy Bonds. "Even they must admit we outplayed them but they still went away with a point."

Graham's decision to pair Stephen Morrow – starting for the first time since breaking his arm in Coca-Cola Cup celebrations seven months earlier – and fellow defender Martin Keown in the centre of midfield suggested all-out attack would not be Arsenal's policy at Upton Park.

But Graham insisted it was a measure forced upon him. David Hillier and Ray Parlour were in bed with flu, Ian Selley had pulled out with the bug earlier that day, Tony Adams was still recovering and John Jensen was unavailable. So Andy Linighan had been asked to play although injured.

Linighan's condition could only have been worsened by the darting runs of Morley. Twice in the first half West Ham should have taken the lead as Ian Bishop's perceptive passing found gaps in the Arsenal defence.

Lee Chapman also had a series of headed opportunities that came to nothing and Burrows had a long-distance drive tipped over the bar by Seaman. Apart from a first-half shot from Anders Limpar, replaced at half-time, Arsenal hardly got a look at goal until substitute Kevin Campbell's glancing header in the 73rd minute that was saved by Ludek Miklosko.

League Table After Match

	P	W	D	L	F	A	Pts
Man Utd.	16	13	2	1	33	13	41
Blackburn	16	8	5	3	22	15	29
Aston Villa	16	8	5	3	18	13	29
Newcastle	16	8	4	4	31	15	28
Norwich	15	7	6	2	25	13	27
Arsenal	16	7	6	3	15	8	27
Leeds	16	9	6	3	26	19	27
QPR	16	8	2	6	28	22	26
Liverpool	15	7	2	6	23	15	23
Tottenham	16	5	6	5	21	17	21
Wimbledon	16	5	6	5	18	23	21
West Ham	16	5	5	6	11	10	20
Coventry	16	4	8	4	17	19	20
Everton	16	6	2	8	18	22	20
Ipswich	16	4	6	6	15	22	18
Sheffield Wed	16	3	8	5	24	24	17
Man City	16	3	7	6	15	17	16
Chelsea	16	3	5	8	11	18	14
Southampton	16	4	2	10	18	26	14
Sheffield Utd	16	2	6	8	17	28	12
Oldham	16	2	5	9	10	27	11
Swindon	16	1	6	9	14	35	9

November 27

ARSENAL 2

NEWCASTLE 1
(Half-time score: 1-0)

Arsenal: Seaman, Dixon, Bould, Morrow, Winterburn, McGoldrick, Keown, Merson, Jensen, Wright, Smith.
Subs: Campbell, Davis, Miller.
Newcastle: Hooper, Venison, Scott, Watson, Elliott, Lee, Bracewell, Sellars, Clark, Cole, Beardsley.
Subs: Howey, Mathie, Srnicek.
Booking: Arsenal: Bould (foul).
Scorers: Arsenal: Wright 15, Smith 60; Newcastle: Beardsley 61.
Referee: A Gunn (Sussex)
Attendance: 36,091

All the pre-match talk was of young Andy Cole's return to Highbury. In the event all the praise was heaped on Ian Wright. "Wright had the pace to cause problems," Newcastle manager Kevin Keegan admitted afterwards. "I told Andy he hadn't had his fairy-tale after all...but it will come."

Arsenal's new North (or Clock) End stand was opened for the game, completing Highbury's renovation into a 39,060 all-seater stadium with giant video screens at either end.

Cole buzzed busily in the opening minutes but a timely tackle by Lee Dixon robbed him of his one meaningful chance in the game. Wright was the first to strike as he proved who was the Highbury master. A corner from Steve Morrow was back-headed by Steve Bould and Wright pounced for his 17th goal of the season as Lee Clark tried desperately to save on the line.

Peter Beardsley prodded and probed at the Arsenal defence but

was unable to find the lethal touch which had helped Cole score 22 goals so far in the season. Wright had a second chance with a header in front of goal from Merson's corner but this time he was well off target.

Alan Smith headed Arsenal's second when Bould touched on a Merson corner and a minute later Newcastle had breached the tough Arsenal defence when, after neat work from Cole, Beardsley picked his spot with clinical care.

England's failure to qualify for the World Cup was briefly forgotten as the game flowed with a style and a strength that thrilled the packed crowd. Newcastle, who came into the match on the back of four successive victories, continued to play their passing game. But it was Arsenal who remained the more dangerous.

Smith missed a header and Wright, after skipping past two defenders, had a shot turned away by Mike Hooper.

Below, Left: Top Gunner: Wright pounces to give Arsenal an early lead

League Table After Match

	P	W	D	L	F	A	Pts
Man Utd.	17	14	2	1	34	13	44
Leeds.	17	8	6	3	29	19	30
Arsenal	17	8	6	3	17	9	30
Blackburn	17	8	5	4	22	16	29
Aston Villa	17	8	5	4	19	15	29
Newcastle	17	8	4	5	32	17	28
Norwich	16	7	6	3	25	16	27
QPR	17	8	3	6	29	23	27
Liverpool	16	8	2	6	24	16	26
Tottenham	17	5	7	5	22	18	22
Wimbledon	17	5	7	5	19	24	22
Everton	17	6	3	8	19	23	21
Ipswich	17	5	6	6	16	22	21
Sheffield Wed	17	4	8	5	27	25	20
Coventry	17	4	8	5	17	20	20
West Ham	16	5	5	6	11	10	20
Man City	17	3	7	7	16	20	16
Sheffield Utd.	17	3	6	8	18	28	15
Southampton	16	4	2	10	18	26	14
Chelsea	17	3	5	9	11	19	14
Oldham	17	3	5	9	12	28	14
Swindon	17	1	6	10	14	38	9

November 30

ARSENAL 0

ASTON VILLA 1
(Half-time score: 0-1)

Arsenal: Seaman, Dixon (Davis), Keown, Bould, Winterburn, McGoldrick, Morrow, Jensen, Merson, Wright, Smith.
Sub: Miller.
Aston Villa: Bosnich, Barrett, Teale, McGrath, Cox, Houghton, Richardson, Townsend, Parker, Saunders, Atkinson.
Subs: Daley, Whittingham, Spink.
Scorer: Villa: Atkinson 4.
Referee: R Hart (Bishop Auckland)
Attendance: 26,453

FOURTH ROUND

It was not a birthday that George Graham will choose to remember. Arsenal's 25-game unbeaten cup run, stretching back 23 months to their shock FA Cup defeat by lowly Wrexham in January 1992, came to a dismal end with a sub-standard performance and defeat to a lone goal by Dalian Atkinson.

A glum Graham said afterwards: "We lost because they were the better team and we had too many players below par. There are no complaints."

Villa had notched victory over Arsenal in the League three weeks earlier in the final minute and they virtually carried on where they had left off by taking the lead after only four minutes.

With Tony Adams fit enough only for a reserve-team run-out and fellow flu victim Andy Linighan an absentee, Villa were under orders to strike early into the heart of Arsenal's defensive partnership of Martin Keown and Steve Bould.

Little more than 48 hours earlier Atkinson had been a virtual outcast when his slack pass had presented Liverpool with their match-winning opportunity. Now he more than made amends, pouncing on a pass from Dean Saunders to expose the limitations of Keown and Bould and shoot under Seaman's diving body.

Villa manager Ron Atkinson, delighted with his namesake's contribution, still demanded more. "He should be up there with the Shearers, the Ferdinands and the Coles. He has the ability to be one of the top three players in the world, never mind just this country."

Manager Atkinson also maintained that a linesman wrongly denied Villa a second goal eight minutes before half-time. The flag was waving as Saunders shot into the net when it seemed Nigel Winterburn was playing him onside.

Arsenal's negative looking midfield of John Jensen and Stephen Morrow failed to get them rolling in return. And on the rare occasions they did get the ball forward there was always the formidable barrier of defender Paul McGrath and goalkeeper Mark Bosnich.

Not until the final 15 minutes, when desperation was creeping into their play, did Arsenal really trouble Villa. Then Morrow, the unlikely Coca-Cola Cup hero at Wembley seven months earlier, forced Bosnich into a superb save with a 20-yard left-foot drive.

December 4

Arsenal arrived at Highfield Road boasting seven consecutive clean sheets and left in a shroud of disappointment. "It was a poor performance," said George Graham. "They had more desire than us all over the pitch and that hurt me."

Mick Quinn, Coventry's roly-poly striker who ambushed Arsenal with a hat-trick on the opening day of the season, struck the winner 11 minutes from time to give Coventry a rare double.

Quinn had been listed at 5-1 to score the first goal in this return match and those who had backed him were counting their money as Sean Flynn robbed Nigel Winterburn to send Quinn away. Not a man renowned for his blinding pace, the chubby Quinn doggedly drew clear of Martin Keown and his accuracy of shot beat Seaman.

It was only the 10th Premiership goal conceded by Seaman and Quinn had scored four of them. He might have had more. Three times early on the big Arsenal goalkeeper had to react brilliantly to deny him.

Quinn's eagerness to make Arsenal and Seaman suffer again brought an angry response from his colleague David Rennie when Quinn went for his fourth attempt. It sailed wide with Rennie unmarked five yards away and the goal gaping. But all was forgiven as Quinn delivered the winner and the first points for Phil Neal since being appointed manager of Coventry.

Seaman needed to be alert a minute later when Quinn fed Roy Wegerle and his firm shot was parried by the England goalkeeper. He was also called upon to react with courage and speed to stop Flynn, Willie Boland and Rennie.

Arsenal, by contrast, lacked even the semblance of passion in their team. They failed to entertain and lacked endeavour. Their flickering attack only rarely troubled Steve Ogrizovic who stretched to save from Paul Merson, Paul Davis and Ian Wright.

Arsenal's frustration brought them four bookings: Lee Dixon, Selley, Winterburn and Wright.

"I bet Wrighty wishes he had my supply of ammo," joked Quinn afterwards."I feel a bit sorry for him."

COVENTRY 1
ARSENAL 0
(Half-time score: 0-0)

Coventry: Ogrizovic, Atherton, Morgan, Rennie, Babb, Boland, Flynn, Darby, Wegerle, Quinn, Ndlovu.
Subs: J Williams, Marsden, Gould.
Arsenal: Seaman, Dixon, Keown, Adams (Bould), Winterburn, McGoldrick (Campbell), Davis, Selley, Merson, Wright, Smith.
Sub: Miller.
Bookings: Coventry: Darby (foul); Arsenal: Dixon (foul), Selley (foul), Wright (foul), Winterburn (foul).
Scorer: Coventry: Quinn 79.
Referee: R Hart (Bishop Auckland)
Attendance: 12,722

League Table After Match

	P	W	D	L	F	A	Pts
Man Utd.	18	14	3	1	36	15	45
Leeds.	18	9	6	3	32	21	33
Newcastle	18	9	4	5	34	18	31
Arsenal	18	8	6	4	17	10	30
Aston Villa	18	8	6	4	21	17	30
Blackburn	17	8	5	4	22	16	29
Norwich	17	7	7	3	27	18	28
QPR	18	8	4	6	31	25	28
Liverpool	17	8	2	7	25	19	26
West Ham	18	7	5	6	15	17	26
Everton	18	7	3	8	20	23	24
Sheffield Wed	18	5	8	5	30	26	23
Coventry	18	5	8	5	18	20	23
Tottenham	18	5	7	6	23	20	22
Wimbledon	18	5	7	6	20	26	22
Ipswich	18	5	7	6	16	22	22
Man City	18	3	7	8	18	23	16
Sheffield Utd	18	3	7	8	18	28	16
Oldham	18	3	6	9	12	28	15
Chelsea	17	3	5	9	11	19	14
Southampton	18	4	2	12	18	29	14
Swindon	18	1	7	10	14	38	10

December 6

ARSENAL 1

TOTTENHAM 1
(Half-time score: 0-1)

Arsenal: Seaman, Dixon, Keown, Adams, Bould, Limpar, Jensen, Selley, Merson, Smith (Campbell), Wright.
Subs: Morrow, Miller.
Tottenham: Thorstvedt, Campbell, Calderwood, Sedgley, Edinburgh, Hazard, Anderton, Caskey, Samways, Dozzell, Kerslake.
Subs: Hendry, Austin, Walker.
Booking: Tottenham: Samways (dissent).
Scorers: Arsenal: Wright 64; Tottenham: Anderton 25.
Referee: P Don (Hanworth Park)
Attendance: 35,669

George Graham threatened an Arsenal shake-up as only an Ian Wright goal saved his spluttering team from their third defeat in a week. Graham, who left out Paul Davis and Eddie McGoldrick from the side that had lost to Coventry, said: "I made changes to try to get some spark, and I'll keep on doing that."

But Arsenal's stop-go form which had seen them virtually concede the championship chase, was clearly frustrating Graham. "The real problem is that we are not consistent enough," he added. "There's no point even talking about the chances of catching Manchester United while that is the case."

These North London confrontations are usually more about pride – and not a little prejudice – but this one was about credibility as well. Arsenal had six days earlier relinquished the Coca-Cola Cup against Aston Villa and the hopes of some end-of-season silverware were diminishing.

Tottenham themselves had gone eight Premiership games without a win, even though they had beaten Blackburn in the Coca-Cola Cup – the prelude to a run which would see them plummet towards relegation trouble.

Initial clashes were, as ever, more emotional than clinical although stand-in striker Sol Campbell gave an Arsenal defence missing the injured Nigel Winterburn some anxiety. Tottenham's neat, quick passing troubled Arsenal and they nearly took a 16th-minute lead when Justin Edinburgh's quick throw-in sent Darren Caskey scampering down the left. His cross was bound for Jason Dozzell until Ian Selley intercepted.

Wright, scorer of the only goal when these two teams met three days into the season at White Hart Lane, was always going to be the chief threat to Tottenham. When Alan Smith headed him into space in the 20th minute both central defenders Colin Calderwood and Steve Sedgley were on hand to block his effort. Immediately afterwards Erik Thorstvedt was needed to make his first save from the recalled Anders Limpar.

But it was Spurs who took a deserved lead through Darren Anderton after 25 minutes following a move of superb simplicity, played at dazzling speed. Mickey Hazard, making his first North

Danger man: Scorer Wright celebrates his equalizer

London derby appearance for eight years since his surprise £500,000 move back to Tottenham from Swindon, pumped the ball upfield. Dozzell headed on and Anderton had the pace and anticipation to cut through an Arsenal defence in which Tony Adams was still suffering after-effects of flu. Ten minutes later Tottenham almost went further ahead. Caskey made contact with Anderton's cross and the ball went close enough to the target to have David Seaman scrambling.

Just when Highbury was getting restless up popped that man Wright again to grab a draw. Limpar provided a clever chipped cross in the 64th minute and there was Wright to smack home a left-foot volley.

It was Wright's 23rd goal of the season, including four for England against San Marino, and his 74th in 105 games for Arsenal since signing for £2.5 million from Crystal Palace in October 1991. Little wonder Graham had just secured his signature on a five-year contract to keep him at Highbury until he is 34.

"The boss gave us a real rollicking at half-time," said Wright afterwards. "I'm just glad I was able to score. It was a great ball from Anders. I let it fall over my shoulder as low as possible before shooting so that I wouldn't sky it."

League Table After Match

	P	W	D	L	F	A	Pts
Man Utd.	19	15	3	1	39	15	48
Leeds.	18	9	6	3	32	21	33
Blackburn	18	9	5	4	24	16	32
Newcastle	18	9	4	5	34	18	31
Arsenal	19	8	7	4	18	11	31
Aston Villa	18	8	6	4	21	17	30
Norwich	17	7	7	3	27	18	28
QPR	18	8	4	6	31	25	28
Liverpool	17	8	2	7	25	19	26
West Ham	18	7	5	6	15	17	26
Everton	18	7	3	8	20	23	24
Sheffield Wed	18	5	8	5	30	26	23
Tottenham	19	5	8	6	24	21	23
Coventry	18	5	8	5	18	20	23
Wimbledon	18	5	7	6	20	26	22
Ipswich	18	5	7	6	16	22	22
Oldham	19	4	6	9	14	29	18
Man City	18	3	7	8	18	23	16
Sheffield Utd.	19	3	7	9	18	31	16
Chelsea	18	3	5	10	11	21	14
Southampton	18	4	2	12	18	29	14
Swindon	19	1	7	11	15	40	10

December 12

ARSENAL 1

SHEFFIELD WEDNESDAY 0
(Half-time score: 0-0)

Arsenal: Miller, Dixon, Morrow, Selley, Adams, Keown (Bould), Jensen, Wright, Smith, Merson (Campbell), Limpar.
Sub: Will.
Sheffield Wed: Pressman, Nilsson, Walker, Palmer, Worthington, Bart-Williams, Hyde, Jones, Coleman, Jemson, Bright.
Subs: Poric, Pearce, Key.
Scorer: Arsenal: Wright 90.
Referee: D Gallagher (Banbury)
Attendance: 22,026

League Table After Match

	P	W	D	L	F	A	Pts
Man Utd.	20	15	4	1	40	16	49
Leeds.	19	10	6	3	33	21	36
Blackburn	19	10	5	4	26	17	35
Arsenal	20	9	7	4	19	11	34
Newcastle	19	9	5	5	35	19	32
QPR	20	9	4	7	34	28	31
Aston Villa	20	8	7	5	23	20	31
Liverpool	19	9	3	7	30	23	30
West Ham	20	8	5	7	18	20	29
Norwich	17	7	7	3	27	18	28
Tottenham	20	6	8	6	26	21	26
Ipswich	20	6	8	6	18	23	26
Everton	20	7	4	9	20	24	25
Wimbledon	19	6	7	6	21	26	25
Sheffield Wed	20	5	9	6	32	29	24
Coventry	19	5	8	6	20	23	23
Man City	20	4	7	9	19	25	19
Oldham	20	4	6	10	15	31	18
Sheffield Utd	20	3	8	9	18	31	17
Chelsea	19	3	6	10	12	22	15
Southampton	20	4	2	14	18	31	14
Swindon	20	1	8	11	17	42	11

Ian Wright spent 90 minutes in Des Walker's custody and then a lapse which would have embarrassed Group Four set him free at Highbury. The long winter afternoon had proved a frustrating time for Arsenal but all that was forgotten as Wright slipped Walker's handcuffs to give Arsenal the most unlikely of victories.

This was the sixth meeting between the sides in 1993, including three Wembley finals, and Wednesday must have left wondering exactly what they have to do to beat Arsenal. Even allowing for their carelessness in the penalty area – Mark Bright in particular being wildly wasteful – they looked set to stretch their unbeaten run to 13 matches.

But with more than 91 minutes on the clock Arsenal goalkeeper Alan Miller began the attack which was to change the match. In one powerful movement he threw the ball to Stephen Morrow almost on the halfway line. Morrow hoisted it towards the Wednesday penalty area where Alan Smith helped it on and, for once, Wright had put yardage between himself and Walker to fire a shot into the corner of the net.

Wedneday must have felt like crying. They had tried to impose their football on Arsenal and the skilful Chris Bart-Williams, especially, had brought a touch of sophistication to their forward play.

It was a testament to Wednesday's depth of talent that even without Chris Waddle and Andy Sinton, absentees through flu and injury, they tested an Arsenal defence that had conceded 11 goals in 20 matches. Bright missed a straight-forward headed chance early in the first half and then squandered an even more simple one soon after the break when Martin Keown allowed him an opening.

Nigel Jemson then missed when it seemed easier to score in the 69th minute. All were chances which Wright made them regret not taking. Wednesday manager Trevor Francis said: "It's never a classic when we play Arsenal. We try to impose ourselves on the game and they have their plan to stop us. I was pleased with the way we went about our football but we are disappointed to have had our unbeaten run ended."

December 18

Arsenal had suffered only two defeats in 14 as they travelled to Elland Road and, given their record against Leeds, they had rightly expected that figure to reach 15 when disaster struck from the unlikeliest of sources.

With the game delicately balanced at 1-1, Tony Adams, marshal of the tightest defence in the Premiership, inexplicably nodded a Gary McAllister free-kick past his own goalkeeper.

But if Adams's goal was unworthy of his overall performance, McAllister's opener for Leeds was not. The Leeds skipper ushered in the season of goodwill with one of the best goals he has ever struck after 20 minutes. He chipped the ball over Ian Selley on the edge of the box, drew David Seaman and coolly slotted home off the post.

Arsenal, forced to reshuffle after the withdrawal of flu victims Paul Merson and Martin Keown, were level within minutes. Ian Wright broke down the right and hit a dangerous cross to the far post. John Newsome headed clear but only as far as John Jensen, who knocked the ball back for Kevin Campbell to score from close range.

Arsenal might have had a second but Anders Limpar failed to find his range with two attempts and instead it was Adams who found himself a reluctant addition to the score-sheet.

Leeds's victory was only their second over Arsenal in 14 attempts. "Yes, they have been a pain in the butt for us," said Leeds manager Howard Wilkinson.

George Graham declared himself happy with the performance if not the result. "We created more chances," he said. "If Limpar had had his shooting boots on we would have taken the points."

Defeat left Arsenal in fifth spot, 15 points off the pace. Leeds were second.

LEEDS 2
ARSENAL 1
(Half-time score: 1-1)

Leeds: Beeney, Dorigo, Fairclough, Strachan, Wallace, Deane, McAllister, Hodge, Newsome, Weatherall, Kelly. *Subs:* Rocastle, Sharp, Lukic.
Arsenal: Seaman, Dixon (Morrow), Winterburn, Adams, Campbell, Wright, Smith (Parlour), Bould, Limpar, Jensen, Selley. *Sub:* Miller.
Bookings: Leeds: Newsome (foul); Arsenal: Limpar (foul).
Scorers: Leeds: McAllister 21, Adams (o.g.) 60; Arsenal: Campbell 27.
Referee: K Burge (Tonypandy)
Attendance: 37,515

League Table After Match

	P	W	D	L	F	A	Pts
Man Utd.	21	16	4	1	43	17	52
Leeds.	21	11	6	4	36	24	39
Blackburn	20	11	5	4	28	17	38
Newcastle	20	10	5	5	37	19	35
Arsenal	21	9	7	5	20	13	34
Norwich	19	8	7	4	30	21	31
Liverpool	20	9	4	7	33	26	31
QPR	20	9	4	7	34	28	31
Aston Villa	21	8	7	6	24	23	31
Ipswich	21	7	8	6	20	24	29
West Ham	21	8	5	8	18	25	29
Wimbledon	20	7	7	6	23	26	28
Sheffield Wed	21	6	9	6	37	29	27
Tottenham	21	6	9	6	29	24	27
Everton	21	7	4	10	20	26	25
Coventry	20	5	9	6	21	24	24
Man City	21	4	7	10	19	27	19
Oldham	21	4	7	10	16	32	19
Sheffield Utd	21	3	8	10	18	33	17
Chelsea	19	3	6	10	12	22	15
Southampton	21	4	2	15	19	33	14
Swindon	21	2	8	11	19	43	14

December 27

(Half-time score: 0-2)

Arsenal: Seaman, Dixon, Winterburn, Parlour (Merson), Bould, Adams (Keown), Jensen, Wright, Campbell, Hillier, McGoldrick.
Sub: Miller.
Swindon: Digby, Fenwick, Taylor, Whitbread, Bodin, Ling, Horlock, Maskell, Moncur, Mutch, Scott.
Subs: Summerbee, Fjortoft, Hammond.
Bookings: Arsenal: Wright (foul), Hillier (foul); Swindon: Moncur (foul).
Scorers: Arsenal: Campbell 19, 26, 68, Wright 89.
Referee: S Lodge (S. Yorks)
Attendance: 17,651

Kevin Campbell scored a brilliant hat-trick to demolish Swindon...and even then failed to upstage Ian Wright. The Arsenal striking pair were in devastating form, but it was Wright's fantastic last-minute goal which will live in the memory.

The England ace turned 35 yards from goal and, with Swindon goalkeeper Fraser Digby no more than five yards off his line, chipped the ball perfectly into the top corner. Swindon manager John Gorman could only say with admiration: "I've never seen a better striker than Ian Wright. It was a brilliant goal. The only consolation for us was that Arsenal were extra special today. It was the best team performance against us by any team this season, including Manchester United."

The Gunners, having blown hot and cold all season, caught fire on this freezing day. The only surprise was that it took them 19 minutes to profit from Swindon's suicidal offside tactics. Then Ray Parlour's through-ball released Wright and his cross was poked home by Campbell at the far post.

Campbell had looked offside but there could be little sympathy for a team gambling on such risky tactics against the pace of the Arsenal strike-force and Gorman was quick to dissociate himself from the ploy. "I can assure you it wasn't on instructions from me," he said afterwards. "I don't like the tactic because it's too much of a gamble."

Wright made the second goal for Campbell with a superbly timed pass forward in the 26th minute. Campbell raced clear to beat the defenceless Digby easily.

The Gunners spurned a series of further clear chances before Campbell completed his hat-trick after 68 minutes, guiding home a cross from Parlour. Wright, booked for a foolish foul on Nicky Summerbee, finished the rout with his spectacular strike.

Graham had left out Paul Merson and Anders Limpar as he continued his mix-and-match selection policy of recent weeks. "The blend was right today," he said, "but overall this season I've been disappointed."

Campbell's hat-trick – his second of the season following the one against Ipswich – took his goal tally to 12. "Campbell was out-

standing," said Graham. "He has the ability and the strength and, if he has the desire as well, he can be a real handful for anybody."

Three of a kind: Kevin Campbell sends Fraser Digby the wrong way for his hat-trick

League Table After Match

	P	W	D	L	F	A	Pts
Man Utd.	22	16	5	1	44	18	53
Leeds.	22	11	7	4	37	25	40
Blackburn	21	11	6	4	29	18	39
Arsenal	22	10	7	5	24	13	37
Newcastle	21	10	6	5	38	20	36
Norwich	20	9	7	4	33	22	34
QPR	21	10	4	7	36	28	34
Liverpool	21	9	5	7	33	26	32
Aston Villa	21	8	7	6	24	23	31
Sheffield Wed	22	7	9	6	39	29	30
Ipswich	22	7	9	6	21	25	30
West Ham	22	8	6	8	19	26	30
Wimbledon	21	7	7	7	24	28	28
Tottenham	22	6	9	7	30	27	27
Coventry	21	6	9	6	23	25	27
Everton	22	7	4	11	20	28	25
Man City	21	4	7	10	19	27	19
Oldham	22	4	7	11	16	34	19
Sheffield Utd.	22	3	9	10	18	33	18
Southampton	22	5	2	15	22	34	17
Chelsea	20	3	6	11	13	25	15
Swindon	22	2	8	12	19	47	14

December 29

ARSENAL 3

SHEFFIELD UNITED 0
(Half-time score: 2-0)

Arsenal: Seaman, Dixon, Bould, Adams, Winterburn, Parlour (Keown), Jensen, McGoldrick, Hillier, Wright (Merson), Campbell.
Sub: Miller.
Sheffield Utd: Kelly, Wirmola, Beesley, Rogers, Whitehouse, Hoyland, Scott, Bradshaw, Nilsen, Davison, Flo.
Subs: Hodges, Cork, Muggleton.
Scorers: Arsenal: Campbell 11, 55, Wright 40.
Referee: R Milford (Bristol)
Attendance: 27,035

Kevin Campbell maintained his goal surge with another two as Arsenal set sail for the New Year with fresh optimism. There was another one, too, for Ian Wright and once again his was the most spectacular strike of the night.

It was another Highbury horror show for Sheffield United. Dave Bassett's men had gone 10 hours all but two minutes without scoring by the end of the game and at this stage in the season Campbell and Wright had scored twice as many goals between them as the whole of the United team.

Campbell's new-found confidence was obvious as he thumped Arsenal into an 11th-minute lead. Wright was screaming for a cross as Campbell burst down the left side of the penalty area from David Hillier's pass. But the cross never came. Instead Campbell struck a left-foot shot that cannoned off the far post into the net.

George Graham had decided to stick with the side that overwhelmed Swindon, leaving Paul Merson on the bench until the last 10 minutes. United were no better equipped to deal with Arsenal's direct approach than Swindon, even though Bassett elected to play with five men in a line across his defence until half-time.

Carl Bradshaw and Jonas Wirmola were both powerless to stop Wright as he spun on the angle of the penalty box and let fly with his right foot for the second goal which Bassett described as "sheer quality". Campbell reclaimed the starring role 11 minutes after the break when David Seaman's long clearance bounced over United's defenders. All Campbell had to do was race forward and place his shot past Alan Kelly.

Luckily for Bassett, Campbell's aim was not always as good. Once he broke clear but veered too far to the left and shot wide. Wright, again watching in the middle, was not amused.

Merson's first touch after arriving as substitute presented Campbell with the opportunity to score his second hat-trick inside three days. This time the shot blazed high over the bar.

But Bassett, who saw first Paul Rogers shoot weakly after a David Seaman mistake and then Steve Bould clear off his line from Andy Scott, could only envy Arsenal's striking strength. "We couldn't hit a cow's backside with a banjo," he lamented.

What a double act! Arsenal goal heroes Wright and Campbell go through their victory routine

Graham was in slightly more upbeat mood. "I'm very pleased for Kevin," he found himself saying for the second match in succession. "The crowd have had a bit of a go at him because he's not scored that many goals at home. He's always had all the qualities. It's just a matter of believing in himself. He's powerful, quick, strong and has a good touch. As for him being greedy, I was delighted to see it."

League Table After Match

	P	W	D	L	F	A	Pts
Man Utd.	23	17	5	1	49	20	56
Blackburn	22	12	6	4	31	18	42
Leeds.	23	11	8	4	38	26	41
Arsenal	23	11	7	5	27	13	40
Newcastle	22	10	6	6	38	21	36
QPR	22	10	5	7	37	29	35
Norwich	21	9	7	5	34	24	34
Aston Villa	22	9	7	6	26	24	34
Liverpool	22	9	6	7	34	27	33
Sheffield Wed	23	7	10	6	42	32	31
Tottenham	23	7	9	7	33	28	30
Ipswich	22	7	9	6	21	25	30
West Ham	23	8	6	9	20	29	30
Wimbledon	22	7	8	7	25	29	29
Coventry	21	6	9	6	23	25	27
Everton	23	7	4	12	20	30	25
Man City	22	4	8	10	20	28	20
Oldham	23	4	7	12	18	39	19
Chelsea	21	4	6	11	14	25	18
Southampton	23	5	3	15	23	35	18
Sheffield Utd.	23	3	9	11	18	36	18
Swindon	23	2	9	12	22	50	15

January 1

WIMBLEDON 0

ARSENAL 3
(Half-time score: 0-2)

Wimbledon: Segers, Barton, Jones, Blackwell, Earle, Fitzgerald, Fashanu, Holdsworth, Fear, Ardley, Elkins.
Sub: Clarke, Berry, Sullivan.
Arsenal: Seaman, Dixon (Keown), Winterburn, Parlour, Bould, Adams, Jensen (Merson), Wright, Campbell, Hillier, McGoldrick.
Sub: Miller.
Scorers Arsenal: Campbell 18, Parlour 23, Wright 55.
Referee: G Ashby (Worcester)
Attendance: 16,584

League Table After Match

	P	W	D	L	F	A	Pts
Man Utd.	24	17	6	1	49	20	57
Blackburn	23	13	6	4	32	18	45
Arsenal...........	24	12	7	5	30	13	43
Leeds.............	24	11	9	4	38	26	42
Newcastle........	23	11	6	6	40	21	39
Norwich...........	22	10	7	5	35	24	37
Liverpool.........	23	10	6	7	36	28	36
QPR	23	10	5	8	38	31	35
Sheffield Wed ..	24	8	10	6	44	33	34
Aston Villa	23	9	7	7	26	25	34
West Ham........	24	9	6	9	21	29	33
Tottenham........	24	7	9	8	34	30	30
Coventry.........	22	7	9	6	25	27	30
Ipswich	23	7	9	7	22	27	30
Wimbledon	23	7	8	8	25	32	29
Everton	24	7	4	13	20	31	25
Chelsea	22	5	6	11	17	26	21
Sheffield Utd....	24	4	9	11	20	37	21
Man City........	23	4	8	11	20	30	20
Oldham...........	24	4	7	13	19	41	19
Southampton ...	24	5	3	16	23	36	18
Swindon	24	2	9	13	23	53	15

Arsenal's England goalkeeper David Seaman, after a holiday spell of three wins with 10 goals scored and none conceded, looked at the gap created by Manchester United at the top of the Premiership and said: "It's certainly not beyond us to catch United.

"We're in the kind of form that suggests we can close the gap. We will not give up until it's a lost cause. We'll put pressure on United and see that happens. If they continue to drop points they will start looking over their shoulders."

Wimbledon, a team so often defying the odds, were not about to argue. Their renowned resilience and spirit had been broken with some ease by Arsenal.

A sudden goal feast, with Kevin Campbell at last providing scoring support for Ian Wright, gave Arsenal heart for the Championship chase but manager George Graham and Seaman were equally encouraged by the team's tightness at the other end of the pitch.

"We're looking more solid, but maybe not as exciting without Paul Merson and Anders Limpar," admitted Graham. "Wimbledon are a better team than people give them credit for and to beat them 3-0 is a good result."

In terms of entertainment value this contest was over after two Arsenal goals in a five-minute first-half spell.

Campbell, with his seventh in four games, headed the first after 19 minutes, then Ray Parlour hit another. Campbell might have added to the tally before the break with Wimbledon struggling to ruffle Arsenal's ever-growing composure.

Had Dean Blackwell's 52nd-minute header from a cross by substitute Andy Clarke been accurate, the picture might have changed. But Wright sneaked between hesitant Wimbledon defenders three minutes later to notch his 22nd goal of the season and end all doubt.

John Fashanu should have given Wimbledon's defeat a respectable gloss, but he wasted two late chances.

January 3

Arsenal's promise to turn the screw on Manchester United in the Premiership finished with them losing the screwdriver. Put another way, just when they had threatened to construct a serious challenge after scoring 10 goals in three games, the Londoners ran out of building materials.

This was a disappointing end to what had promised to be a productive seasonal holiday programme. With Blackburn's game against Wimbledon postponed, there was no need for Alex Ferguson to peer over his shoulder as Arsenal keeper David Seaman had suggested he might have to.

Seaman did his best to keep the pressure on United with another clean sheet, but Ian Wright and Kevin Campbell failed to keep their side of the bargain.

That in part was due to the excellence of defender Steve Yates, educated by Rangers boss Gerry Francis at Bristol Rovers. He played 22-goal Wright as well as any defender this season.

Rangers had already been doing their bit to keep United in check, having held Leeds to a point over Christmas.

Campbell, whose seven goals in four games had provided the thrust for the club's surge into third place, missed two chances in the first 14 minutes. He headed against the bar from Eddie McGoldrick's fourth-minute corner and should have made more of his opening 10 minutes later when he was clean through on Jan Stejskal. But his shot hit the Rangers keeper.

It was a frustrating afternoon for Ray Parlour, the most productive player on the pitch, whose service from the right was near to exemplary. Less might be said of Rangers' own creativity because they were largely overwhelmed in midfield by the industry of John Jensen and David Hillier.

Les Ferdinand, strangely subdued, provoked the best save of the match from Seaman with a shot that skidded off the surface.

Francis said: "For the first 25 minutes we looked as if we were poorly. But after that I thought we coped well." Rangers usually do against Arsenal. These sides have played four goalless draws in their last five meetings.

But the only person smiling after this one was up in Manchester.

ARSENAL 0
QPR 0

Arsenal: Seaman, Dixon, Winterburn, Parlour, Bould, Adams, Jensen (Keown), Wright, Campbell, Hillier, McGoldrick.
Subs: Merson, Miller.
QPR: Stejskal, Bardsley, Wilson, Wilkins, Yates, Peacock, Sinclair, Barker, Ferdinand, Penrice, Meaker.
Subs: Impey, Brevett, Roberts.
Bookings: Arsenal: Wright (foul); QPR: Penrice (foul).
Referee: J Borrett (Norfolk)
Attendance: 25,642

League Table After Match

	P	W	D	L	F	A	Pts
Man Utd.	25	17	7	1	52	23	58
Blackburn	23	13	6	4	32	18	45
Arsenal	25	12	8	5	30	13	44
Newcastle	24	12	6	6	42	22	42
Leeds	24	11	9	4	38	26	42
Sheffield Wed	25	9	10	6	45	33	37
Norwich	23	10	7	6	36	26	37
Liverpool	24	10	7	7	39	31	37
QPR	24	10	6	8	38	31	36
Aston Villa	23	9	7	7	26	25	34
West Ham	25	9	7	9	21	29	34
Coventry	23	7	10	6	26	27	31
Tottenham	25	7	9	9	34	31	30
Ipswich	23	7	9	7	22	27	30
Wimbledon	23	7	8	8	25	32	29
Everton	25	7	4	14	22	35	25
Chelsea	23	6	6	11	21	28	24
Sheffield Utd	25	4	10	11	20	37	22
Man City	23	4	8	11	20	30	20
Oldham	24	4	7	13	19	41	19
Southampton	24	5	3	16	23	36	18
Swindon	25	2	10	13	24	54	16

January 10

MILLWALL 0

ARSENAL 1
(Half-time score: 0-0)

Millwall: Keller, Huxford, Thatcher, Roberts, Van Den Hauwe, Stevens, Rae, Verveer, Mitchell, Goodman, Barber.
Subs: Emberson, Moralee, May.
Arsenal: Seaman, Dixon, Winterburn, Adams, Hillier, Bould (Jensen), Keown, Parlour, Wright (Merson), Campbell, McGoldrick.
Sub: Miller.
Bookings: Arsenal: Wright (foul), Bould (foul).
Scorer: Arsenal: Adams 90.
Referee: P Durkin (Portland)
Attendance: 20,093

THIRD ROUND

Tony Adams, the late, late show man, provided the finale once again as Arsenal made a stern if unromantic defence of the FA Cup. It was Adams who had produced the last-minute winner for Arsenal against Tottenham in the semi-final in 1993 and this time he took it even closer to the wire.

The 90 minutes had run out on Millwall's giant electronic scoreboard in their splendid New Den when Adams galloped forwards for one final corner.

Eddie McGoldrick delivered the ball to the heart of the six-yard box and, as American goalkeeper Kasey Keller dropped it under pressure from Paul Merson, Adams was on hand to force it over the line.

It was a dramatic ending for Arsenal and a near disastrous one for Keller who was being watched by the United States assistant manager Timo Liekowski with an eye to World Cup selection.

Otherwise the FA Cup holders had not troubled sociology graduate Keller in a dour struggle which ill-befitted the fine surroundings.

Arsenal smothered Millwall's playmakers Andy Roberts and Etienne Verveer with man-for-man marking by David Hillier and Martin Keown. At the same time Millwall's central defence of Pat Van Den Hauwe and veteran Keith Stevens was doing a sound restrictive job on Kevin Campbell and Ian Wright. Eventually Wright, suffering from a virus, was booked and substituted and would miss the next round against Bolton.

Passes were squandered all over the pitch and, if Arsenal held the edge, it was simply because they were more adept at winning back the ball. Perhaps if Millwall had grasped a chance in the first 30 seconds it would have set up a more enthralling evening, but Keown got his foot in to deflect Dave Mitchell's effort.

Arsenal fashioned a couple of excellent opportunities in the first half but McGoldrick's glancing header was off target and Campbell shot weakly under pressure. Wright, subjected to abuse that brought no credit to the Millwall fans, was a subdued figure and unlucky to be cautioned for a challenge on Ben Thatcher. Steve

*Three's a crowd: Seaman and
Winterburn combine to keep out
Millwall's Verveer*

Bould followed him into Paul Durkin's book for a more sinister
challenge on Mitchell early in the second half.

Arsenal again had the better second-half chances, McGoldrick
supplying one cross for Ray Parlour to volley just over the angle.

After Merson replaced the ailing Wright in the 70th minute
Arsenal carried a more serious threat. Yet the game still seemed to
be heading for a replay when Adams turned on the late show.

January 15

MANCHESTER CITY 0

ARSENAL 0
(Half-time score: 0-0)

Man City: Coton, Edghill, Phelan, Brightwell, Kernaghan, Vonk, Rocastle, Groenendijk, Griffiths, Ingebritsen, Lomas.
Subs: Sheron, Flitcroft.
Arsenal: Seaman, Dixon, Winterburn, Adams, Campbell, Wright, McGoldrick (Merson), Bould, Jensen, (Keown), Hillier, Parlour.
Subs:
Bookings: Man City: Ingebritsen (foul); Arsenal: Winterburn (foul).
Referee: D Allison (Lancaster)
Attendance: 25,642

League Table After Match

	P	W	D	L	F	A	Pts
Man Utd.	26	18	7	1	53	23	61
Blackburn	24	14	6	4	34	19	48
Arsenal	26	12	9	5	30	13	45
Leeds.	25	11	10	4	38	26	43
Newcastle	24	12	6	6	42	22	42
Liverpool	25	11	7	7	42	31	40
Norwich	24	10	8	6	37	27	38
Sheffield Wed	26	9	10	7	46	35	37
Aston Villa	24	10	7	7	29	26	37
QPR	24	10	6	8	38	31	36
West Ham	26	9	7	10	22	32	34
Wimbledon	24	8	8	8	27	33	32
Coventry	24	7	10	7	26	28	31
Ipswich	24	7	10	7	22	27	31
Tottenham	26	7	9	10	34	32	30
Everton	26	8	4	14	28	37	28
Chelsea	24	6	7	11	22	29	25
Sheffield Utd	26	4	10	12	21	39	22
Man City	24	4	9	11	20	30	21
Southampton	25	6	3	16	24	36	21
Oldham	25	4	7	14	19	44	19
Swindon	26	2	10	14	26	60	16

Arsenal boss George Graham bent Ian Wright's eardrums for allowing himself to be shut out by City rookie Richard Edghill. It seemed a bit harsh, especially as the England striker has scored 22 goals in 33 outings this season

Nor did the dressing room diatribe – Graham let rip at his star attacker at the break and full-time – take much account of young Edghill's ice-cool stalking.

Graham complained: "We were sleeping. We just weren't alive in the box. Edghill looks a good player but Ian Wright was below par."

City were buffeted by power politics and injuries and forcibly mixed like a bag of toffees by manager Brian Horton. The Maine Road crisis has produced a few bonuses like the arrival of former Arsenal favourite David Rocastle, the switch to midfield of full-back Terry Phelan and the balance and technique of big defender Michel Vonk up front. Then there is Edghill. Moved to the centre of defence from full-back, he had the pace and ability to confine the most slippery attacker in English football to one shot against the post.

"I'm quick but he matched me," said Wright." I rate Des Walker still the toughest defender to play against but young Edghill wasn't far off his standard. He was so calm. He never seems to get ruffled and that's important in a defender."

Vonk's aerial power tested Arsenal's redoubtable defence early on but not even Paul Merson's early arrival as sub for the injured Eddie McGoldrick sparked the Gunners up front.

Rocastle had words of sympathy for Merson, who continues to tread a tightrope at Highbury. "My advice to him is to keep his head down and get on with it because reputations don't mean much to George," said the star Arsenal sold to Leeds for £2 million.

Niall Quinn, out for the rest of the season after a serious knee injury, was an apprentice at Highbury with Rocastle and enthused: "I couldn't believe it when we got a man of his quality. But my first words in the dressing room were for young Edghill.

"I told him to remember today because not many people will come off the pitch and claim to have done as well as that against Ian Wright."

January 22

If Arsenal sometimes throw up an image of aloofness as cold as those marble halls, you can usually warm your hands on the personality of Wright. He glows with confidence in his own ability, faith in his team and supreme optimism. And Arsenal needed such a personality to lift spirits after the draw with struggling Oldham.

Although scoring his 23rd goal of the season, from the penalty spot, Wright had unusually failed to capitalise on a spate of late opportunities in front of goal. And without his genius Arsenal looked predictable.

Yet, while two points went begging, Arsenal stretched their unbeaten run to seven games and Wright typically refused to concede that Manchester United were inevitable champions. "Not until the last game," he advocated. "They are setting a standard that everybody is going to have to follow – or be embarrassed by. So it is up to the rest to make sure they can stay with them."

It has been suggested that, had Arsenal matched United's financial commitment in the transfer market, the title might be a two-horse race. Certainly Wright looked in need of a more creative background.

But he said: "It might benefit my game if we had a few more creative midfield players. Yet I had four good chances and we're told we don't have the so-called creative players. It is up to me to take the chances. It is up to the individual to do the best he can with the players around him."

Everything about Wright remains positive, even after those wasted chances. "What Oldham might not have in quality they have in commitment and endeavour," he said. "They went in front with a great goal from Graeme Sharp and it gave them a lift. They were always going to be hard to break down. Just because they are down the bottom does not give you the right to win."

Sharp's superb fourth-minute strike was a highlight of a first half in which Arsenal confirmed the thoughts of their critics that they are born lucky. Their stroke of good fortune came in first-half injury-time when Mike Milligan seemed harshly judged to have handled.

Wright smacked home the penalty with the air of someone who knows you make your own luck in this game.

ARSENAL 1

OLDHAM 1
(Half-time score: 1-1)

Arsenal: Seaman, Dixon, Winterburn, Parlour, Bould, Adams, Jensen (Keown), Wright, Campbell, Hillier, McGoldrick (Merson).
Sub: Miller.
Oldham: Hallworth, Fleming, Makin, Pointon, Jobson, Redmond, Bernard, Sharp, McCarthy, Milligan, Holden.
Subs: Gerrard, Pederson, Plamer.
Scorers: Arsenal: Wright (pen) 45; Oldham: Sharp 4.
Referee: P Foakes (Clacton)
Attendance: 26,524

League Table After Match

	P	W	D	L	F	A	Pts
Man Utd.	27	19	7	1	54	23	64
Blackburn	25	15	6	4	36	20	51
Arsenal	27	12	10	5	31	14	46
Newcastle	26	13	6	7	45	25	45
Liverpool	26	12	7	7	44	32	43
Leeds	26	11	10	5	39	28	43
Sheffield Wed	27	10	10	7	49	36	40
QPR	26	11	6	9	40	33	39
Norwich	26	10	8	6	37	27	38
Aston Villa	25	10	8	7	30	27	38
West Ham	26	9	7	10	22	32	34
Wimbledon	25	8	9	8	27	33	33
Ipswich	25	7	11	7	22	27	32
Coventry	25	7	10	8	26	29	31
Tottenham	27	7	9	11	35	34	30
Everton	27	8	4	15	28	38	28
Chelsea	25	6	8	11	23	30	26
Southampton	26	7	3	16	26	37	24
Sheffield Utd.	27	4	10	13	22	42	22
Man City	25	4	9	12	21	32	21
Oldham	26	4	8	14	20	45	20
Swindon	27	3	10	14	28	61	19

BOLTON **2**

ARSENAL **2**
(Half-time score: 1-0)

Bolton: Davison, Brown, Phillips, Kelly, McAteer, Winstanley, Lee, Stubbs, Coyle, McGinlay, Patterson.
Subs: Walker, Burke, Hoult.
Arsenal: Seaman, Dixon, Winterburn, Hillier, Bould, Adams, Keown, Merson, Campbell, Parlour (Smith), Wright.
Subs: Jensen, Miller.
Scorers: Bolton: McAteer 31, Coyle 86; Arsenal: Wright 51, Adams 66.
Referee: T Holbrook (Wolverhampton)
Attendance: 18,891

FOURTH ROUND

Arsenal manager George Graham had known what to expect with Bolton. He had seen them look out on their feet against Everton in the third round only to come roaring back and win the replay.

But it made it no easier to accept when Bolton produced a similar revival for Owen Coyle to hit the 86th-minute equaliser which carried the First Division glory boys towards another big replay night at Highbury.

Coyle had been sprinkling goals throughout Bolton's Cup run since the first round when his two late strikes disposed of non-League Gretna. When John McGinlay headed back a cross from Tony Kelly with four minutes remaining, there was Coyle to continue his amazing streak.

Bruce Rioch's side deserved their second chance if only for their never-say-die spirit which left Arsenal wondering what had hit them during a hectic first half. Jason McAteer, a member of the famous Merseyside boxing family, threatened to put Cup holders Arsenal on the canvas after 31 minutes. Kelly fed the ball through to McGinlay and he set up the 22-year-old midfielder McAteer to slot Bolton's opener through the legs of an embarrassed David Seaman.

The Gunners could have buckled as Wanderers piled on the pressure. Seaman blocked a shot from Coyle, clawed away a header from Phil Brown and was grateful to see David Lee sidefoot across a gaping goal.

Meanwhile Ian Wright, Martin Keown and big Kevin Campbell were all off target when first-half chances beckoned. A stern lecture from Graham at half-time seemed to put that right and Arsenal strode Burnden's bumpy surface with more purpose after the break.

Within six minutes Wright had pounced from six yards on an easy chance after Merson's cross had been deflected into his path. Then, when Nigel Winterburn flung over a 66th-minute free-kick, Tony Adams strode forward to head Arsenal into the lead.

But Bolton were never going to lie down on a night like this and Coyle, a £250,000 recruit from Airdrie, fittingly clinched another huge pay day. "It will be difficult going to Highbury," he said. "But we go there with real hope."

Seaman and Adams sing each other's praises

Graham agreed. "They will come with confidence," he said. "They deserved their equaliser. Their attack gave our back four a lot of problems. They made our lads work harder than our forwards did theirs."

Bolton manager Rioch was full of praise for his team. "The character, attitude and commitment of this team is phenomenal," he said. It was an assessment which would haunt Arsenal in the replay.

February 9

ARSENAL 1

BOLTON 3
(after extra time, full-time score: 1-1)

Arsenal: Seaman, Dixon, Winterburn, Hillier (Keown), Bould, Adams, Parlour, Wright (McGoldrick), Smith, Merson, Campbell.
Sub: Miller.
Bolton: Davison, Brown, Phillips, Kelly, Seagraves, Stubbs, Lee, McAteer, Coyle, McGinlay, Patterson.
Subs: Walker, Burke, Hoult.
Sent off: Arsenal: Keown (two bookings).
Scorers: Arsenal: Smith 36; Bolton: McGinlay 20, McAteer 99, Walker 115.
Referee: G Ashby (Worcs)
Attendance: 33,863

FOURTH ROUND REPLAY

Arsenal had the FA Cup wrested from them by a superb performance from Bruce Rioch's Bolton. Two extra-time goals ensured Arsenal's exit on a night of high drama which saw Martin Keown sent off in the final seconds.

Keown just had time to reach the dug-out before the final whistle signalled massive Bolton celebrations. It was a bizarre dismissal, coming from a second booking when Keown rushed forward to block a free-kick from Tony Kelly which ended up in the back of the net.

Referee Gerald Ashby ordered it to be retaken, which baffled George Graham. "I rate him highly as a referee," he said, "but to be sent off for that seems sad. There's got to be some common sense in the game. The goal should surely have stood."

There was no denying that Bolton deserved their victory as they inflicted Arsenal's first defeat in nine outings. John McGinlay gave them the springboard with a 20th-minute goal headed home from close range after Arsenal failed to clear Mark Patterson's corner.

Arsenal were level after 36 minutes when Lee Dixon's free-kick was nodded forward by Tony Adams for Ian Wright to challenge for possession with goalkeeper Aidan Davison. The ball ran loose and Alan Smith was there to score his first goal since November.

The game thundered into extra time and after 103 minutes Nigel Winterburn made an uncharacteristic but crucial mistake. His back-pass lacked power and fell into the path of Owen Coyle, whose shot rebounded off goalkeeper David Seaman and on to a post. Jason McAteer, following up, gratefully fired the ball home.

Five minutes from the end substitute striker Andy Walker was put clear by David Lee and drove home the third to end any doubts about the outcome. To complete Arsenal's gloom, defender Steve Bould was taken to hospital for X-rays on a suspected stress fracture. "We had enough chances but didn't play well," said Graham. "Two of their goals were presentations, but give Bolton their fair due. And good luck to them."

February 13

Kevin Campbell struck perhaps the simplest goal of his career, but certainly one of the most crucial, as Arsenal restored their morale with a compact display against Norwich.

The big centre-forward had taken the brunt of the fans' abuse after the shock FA Cup defeat against Bolton. But Campbell showed he had the character to answer back in the best fashion.

Arsenal took the lead in the 33rd minute as Campbell made up for the four sitters he had missed against Bolton. Lee Dixon curled over a typical spiralling cross to the far post which deceived Norwich goalkeeper Bryan Gunn. Smith was allowed a free header to knock the ball back and Campbell had only to tap the ball in from two yards.

It was his 16th goal of the season but the first for seven games and reward for manager Graham's faith in keeping him in the side. The Gunners should have gone two up moments later as a superb passing movement out of defence put Nigel Winterburn clear. But the left-back hurriedly slashed his shot across the face of the goal.

Arsenal had restored Paul Davis to the side after a 10-week absence to add subtlety to their midfield. He inspired some classy attacks as Arsenal proved they did not always play Route One.

So it was ironic that Norwich, the culture club, should fashion their equaliser with a classic long-ball strike. Gunn, launched a huge kick upfield and the ever impressive Chris Sutton out-jumped Tony Adams to flick on for Efan Ekoku to ram home a powerful shot from 20 yards.

Ekoku might have won the game a minute later as Norwich surged forward again. This time Sutton delicately chipped the ball into the box but his co-striker sent a diving header just wide. Sutton almost scored himself with a superb long-range shot which David Seaman tipped on to the bar.

But a Norwich victory would have been unjust, especially as the Gunners were convinced they should have had a penalty in the 60th minute when Ray Parlour was pulled down by Rob Newman. "It was an obvious penalty watching it on the TV replay," said Graham. "It only confirmed what everybody in the ground thought."

NORWICH 1

ARSENAL 1
(Half-time score: 0-1)

Norwich: Gunn, Culverhouse, Woodthorpe, Newman, Polston, Goss, Crook, Megson, Bowen, Sutton, Ekoku.
Subs: Eadie, Power, Howie.
Arsenal: Seaman, Dixon, Winterburn, Adams, Bould, Davis, Parlour, Merson, Campbell, Smith, Jensen.
Subs: Keown, Selley, Miller.
Scorers: Norwich: Ekoku 57; Arsenal: Campbell 33.
Referee: R Dilkes (Mossley)
Attendance: 17,667

League Table After Match

	P	W	D	L	F	A	Pts
Man Utd.	28	20	7	1	57	25	67
Blackburn	27	17	6	4	41	20	57
Arsenal	28	12	11	5	32	15	47
Newcastle	27	13	6	8	47	29	45
Liverpool	28	12	8	8	48	38	44
Aston Villa	27	12	8	8	36	27	44
Sheffield Wed	28	11	10	7	52	37	43
Leeds	27	11	10	6	39	29	43
Norwich	27	10	11	6	43	33	41
QPR	27	11	6	10	42	36	39
Wimbledon	27	9	9	9	31	38	36
West Ham	28	9	9	10	25	35	36
Coventry	28	8	11	9	28	32	35
Ipswich	28	7	12	9	23	30	33
Everton	29	9	5	15	32	40	32
Tottenham	29	7	9	13	36	39	30
Southampton	28	8	3	17	31	41	27
Chelsea	27	6	8	13	26	36	26
Oldham	28	6	8	14	24	47	26
Man City	27	5	10	12	23	33	25
Sheffield Utd	28	4	11	13	22	42	23
Swindon	29	4	10	15	31	67	22

February 19

EVERTON 1

ARSENAL 1
(Half-time score: 0-0)

Everton: Southall, Jackson, Hinchcliffe, Snodin, Watson, Stuart, Beagrie, Rideout, Angell, Moore, Preki.
Subs: Cottee, Horne, Kearton.
Arsenal: Seaman, Dixon, Winterburn, Davis, Adams (Keown), Bould, Jensen (Hillier), Campbell, Smith, Merson, Parlour.
Sub: Miller.
Scorers: Everton: Cottee 81; Arsenal: Merson 56.
Referee: D Allison (Lancaster)
Attendance: 19,891

Paul Merson took centre stage, running through his full repertoire of skill and scoring a stunning goal as poor Kevin Campbell once again found his shooting touch had been left on the training pitch.

Campbell, scorer in the previous match against Norwich, had felt certain that simple tap-in at Carrow Road would bring a change of fortune in front of goal. Instead he missed another series of openings, prompting manager George Graham to lament, "All the chances are falling to Kevin and it's sad to see him suffer. He just has to keep at it."

Campbell's striking partner Alan Smith also sliced a glorious chance wide as Arsenal stacked up a pile of missed opportunities. Merson, in the end, decided to take matters into his own hands after 56 minutes. With Neil Moore standing off him and goalkeeper Neville Southall in no-man's-land Merson lifted a 20-yard chip over both of them and into the net. It was a goal of sheer magic which brought glowing praise fom Everton skipper Dave Watson.

"Merson's playing the Peter Beardsley sort of role, just behind the front two, and he caused us real problems. That finish was unbelievable. He was superb and personally I'm sure he could do it for England, too."

But Merson, who had not managed a Premier League goal since September, remained modest amid the plaudits. "Im enjoying my new role," he said, "and I'm just concentrating on staying in the Arsenal team. I had a couple of bad games and was left out for eight matches. I don't want that to happen again."

Merson admitted he had been pleased by his impudent strike. "It was a special goal, one of my best," he said, "but I'd rather have 20 tap-ins than just one like that every few months. Neville wasn't far off his line. I just saw a small gap and had a go."

The game should have been beyond Everton long before Merson struck. How desperately Arsenal missed the injured Ian Wright, sitting out the match in the stand.

As chance after chance went begging, so Everton were allowed to retrieve a point. Tony Cottee, who had been in conflict with manager Mike Walker after being left out of the side against Ipswich

'A Kick Up The Arse.'

Paul Merson takes control of the Blackburn midfield.

Top Gun: Adams heads the winner against Torino in the Cup Winners' Cup quarter final.

A delighted Merson salutes the crowd.

Jamie Redknapp chases Merson in vain.

No holding back - Wright is unstoppable against Liverpool.

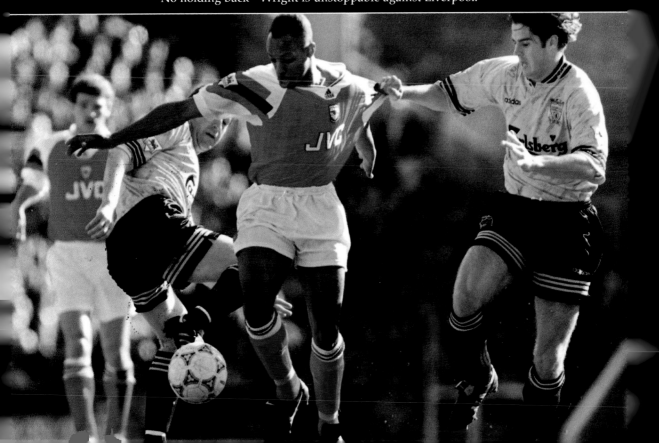

Merson and Jensen put their hands together for a great goal.

Wright keeps his eye on the ball.

Peerless Parlour leaves Lawrie Sanchez floored.

Smith soars to sink Swindon.

Wright down . . .

. . . and out.

The watertight Arsenal defence stops goals leaking in.

Gunning for victory.

The hard man in winning mood.

The battle of Copenhagen - Paul Davis shows his fighting qualities.

Standing room only.

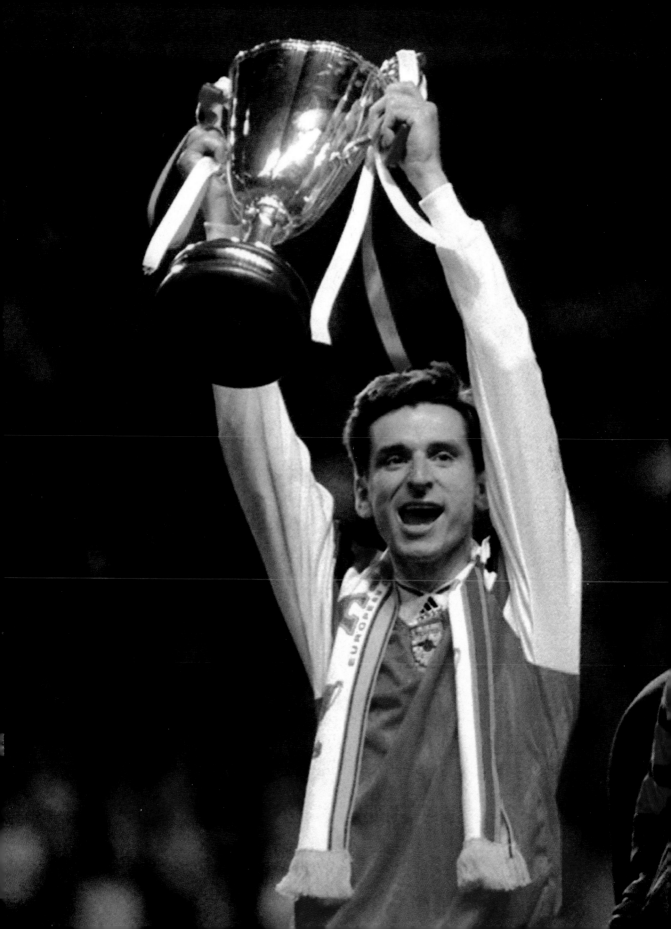

Paul Merson: a goal of sheer magic

the week before, made a return as 72nd-minute substitute. And within 10 minutes he had equalised, making the most of a moment's hesitation in the Arsenal defence to shoot home from eight yards.

League Table After Match

	P	W	D	L	F	A	Pts
Man Utd.	28	20	7	1	57	25	67
Blackburn	28	18	6	4	42	20	60
Arsenal	29	12	12	5	33	16	48
Leeds	28	12	10	6	41	29	46
Newcastle	28	13	6	9	47	30	45
Aston Villa	27	12	8	7	36	27	44
Liverpool	29	12	8	9	48	40	44
Sheffield Wed	28	11	10	7	52	37	43
Norwich	28	10	12	6	46	36	42
QPR	27	11	6	10	42	36	39
Coventry	29	9	11	9	32	32	38
Wimbledon	27	9	9	9	31	38	36
West Ham	28	9	9	10	25	35	36
Ipswich	28	7	12	9	23	30	33
Everton	30	9	6	15	33	41	33
Tottenham	29	7	9	13	36	39	30
Southampton	28	8	3	17	31	41	27
Chelsea	27	6	8	13	26	36	26
Oldham	28	6	8	14	24	47	26
Man City	28	5	10	13	23	37	25
Sheffield Utd.	28	4	11	13	22	42	23
Swindon	30	4	11	15	34	70	23

February 26

ARSENAL 1

BLACKBURN 0
(Half-time score: 0-0)

Arsenal: Seaman, Dixon, Winterburn, Davis, Adams, Bould, Jensen, Campbell, Smith, Merson, Parlour.
Subs: Linighan, Hillier, Will.
Blackburn: Flowers, May, Moran, Berg, Le Saux, Ripley, Batty, Marker, Wilcox, Shearer, Gallacher.
Subs: Morrison, Atkins, Mimms.
Scorer: Arsenal: Merson 73.
Referee: J Worrall (Warrington)
Attendance: 35,030

Even without Ian Wright Arsenal looked more like championship contenders than Blackburn. "That's the first time we have looked second best all season," said Blackburn manager Kenny Dalglish. "They were sharper, brighter and stronger than us. We got what we deserved."

It was Blackburn's first defeat in 13 games and they were made to look second-rate by a disciplined Arsenal performance. Their misery was compounded by a dreadful injury to Kevin Gallacher who suffered a triple fracture of his right leg in an accidental collision with Steve Bould after 26 minutes.

A couple of days before the match George Graham announced that he was looking for a midfield general. Paul Davis must have been listening for he provided some crisp, penetrative passing.

But, if Arsenal looked stronger in the area where they had been weak, they lacked the break of the ball up front. Wright, still suffering from a hamstring strain, was much missed.

Tony Adams was a tower at the back and, along with Bould, succeeded in forcing Alan Shearer to endure his least effective game for many a week.

Davis gave Arsenal their best moment of the first half when his perfectly chiselled free-kick found the normally reliable head of Alan Smith, who this time just missed. Arsenal continued to build the pressure in the second half and Ray Parlour, whose thrusting runs had been a feature of their play, forced his way through. But he attempted to nutmeg goalkeeper Tim Flowers and was foiled.

The Arsenal goal, when it came, was an excellent one. Smith pulled the ball back from the goal-line and Merson, who had been growing in menace, lifted the roof of the net with a powerful shot. Merson came close to adding a second with a tremendous drive but this time Flowers produced an equally spectacular save.

Graham called it "a tremendous team performance" and added, "I thought we won well by playing good, attractive and effective football." There was a suspicion, though, that Graham was content to win without truly revealing the strength of his hand to the watching spies from Torino.

It was left to Merson to sum up the Arsenal philosophy. "The

Class Act ... Merson blasts home Arsenal's winner

vital thing right now is that we don't lose. We have to keep in touch," he said.

Merson again showed the kind of form which could attract England manager Terry Venables who this particular Saturday had chosen to travel elsewhere in his search for "the adaptable, flexible" players he wanted.

Of Venables' other contenders Blackburn's Graeme Le Saux gave another assured display at full-back and Flowers just about edged the goalkeeping honours with Seaman.

The worst performance, strangely, came from the highly respected referee Joe Worrall who failed to stem the stream of niggling fouls early on; consequently a series of more savage transgressions went unpunished later. "It was sad to see one of the best referees have an off-day," said Graham.

League Table After Match

	P	W	D	L	F	A	Pts
Man Utd.	29	20	8	1	59	28	68
Blackburn	30	18	7	5	44	23	61
Arsenal	30	13	12	5	34	16	51
Newcastle	29	14	6	9	51	30	48
Liverpool	30	13	8	9	49	40	47
Leeds.	28	12	10	6	41	29	46
Aston Villa	28	12	9	7	36	27	45
Sheffield Wed	29	11	11	7	53	38	44
Norwich	30	10	14	6	49	39	44
QPR	27	11	6	10	42	36	39
Coventry	31	9	11	11	32	37	38
West Ham	29	9	10	10	27	37	37
Ipswich	29	8	12	9	26	32	36
Wimbledon	28	9	9	10	31	39	36
Everton	30	9	6	15	33	41	33
Tottenham	29	7	9	13	36	39	30
Southampton	29	9	3	17	33	41	30
Man City	30	6	11	13	25	38	29
Chelsea	27	6	8	13	26	36	26
Oldham	28	6	8	14	24	47	26
Sheffield Utd.	29	4	11	14	24	45	23
Swindon	31	4	11	16	35	72	23

March 2

TORINO 0

ARSENAL 0
(Half-time score: 0-0)

Torino: Galli, Sottill, Jarni, Cois, Gregucci, Fusi, Mussi, Fortunato, Silenzi, Francescoli, Venturin.
Subs: Carbone, Sinigaglia, Jorni, Poggi, Carri.
Arsenal: Seaman, Dixon, Winterburn, Davis (Selley), Bould, Adams, Jensen, Campbell, Smith, Merson, Hillier.
Subs: McGoldrick, Keown, Limpar, Miller.
Referee: J Quiniou (France)
Attendance: 32,480

QUARTER FINAL, FIRST LEG

Arsenal proved that no team in England was better equipped to handle Italian football than themselves as they clawed out the defensive draw which gave them real hope of reaching the European Cup Winners' Cup semi-finals.

George Graham may also have harboured hopes of stealing a precious away goal but that possibility dimmed once he had decided that Ian Wright was not sufficiently fit. It was a decision which brought disappointment to Wright and the two men had words after the match.

But Graham was vindicated in the best possible fashion. It is in matches like these that Graham's often maligned tactics stand the severest of examinations. It made for dour viewing with scarcely enough goalmouth action to fill five of the 90 minutes. Yet this was always going to be about guts rather than glory.

Tony Adams resolutely held the defence together while his midfield stifled the threat of the talented Italians. Graham says he views European competition like a game of chess and he had given considerable thought to his opening formation before opting to omit Wright and play Alan Smith as the lone striker with Paul Merson and Kevin Campbell in wide midfield positions.

It made for a formidable midfield barrier but Arsenal's attack, denied the genius of Wright, was a blunt instrument.

Torino's highly talented Enzo Francescoli may be the wrong side of 30 now but he remains one of the game's most charismatic characters and it was to Adams's credit that he was contained. His sole contribution of real menace was a smooth turn inside and a shot over the angle after eight minutes.

Instead it was Arsenal who offered the occasional threat. In the 29th minute Paul Davis's corner was knocked across the goalmouth by Campbell but Adams, sliding in at the far post, was unable to get direction on his shot.

When the Italians did move forward it was mainly through the left-flank thrusts of Robert Jarni. And it was from his 42nd-minute cross that Daniel Fortunato failed to live up to his name by heading wide. Encouraged, Jarni then tried a venomous shot himself which

Kevin Campbell in a typically determined tussle

David Seaman was grateful to hold at the second attempt after the first had spilled from his midriff.

It was a measure of Arsenal's control that the second-half substitutions made by the Italians were in forward positions as they sought the vital goal. That was denied them and Arsenal settled for the draw themselves, substituting their own creative midfield player Paul Davis with young Ian Selley.

Torino manager Emilio Mondonico admitted: "Arsenal are a capable side and showed all their strength against us. We will have to play better in the second leg."

Graham explained Wright's omission: "I was not convinced he was fully fit and he does already have a booking against his name. I was happy with the performance if not with the result. We did lack a cutting edge but there aren't many sides who can come to Italy and dominate as we did.

"Sometimes we in England are in awe of the Italians. I told my players just to go out and express themselves. We know we will have to be patient again in the second leg."

March 5

IPSWICH 1

ARSENAL 5
(Half-time score: 0-3)

Ipswich: Baker, Stockwell, Thompson, Wark, Linighan, Williams, Marshall, Kiwomya, Youds, Palmer, Slater.
Subs: Mason, Guentchev, Morgan.
Arsenal: Seaman, Dixon, Winterburn, Adams, Bould, Hillier (Keown), Selley, Parlour, Limpar (Merson), Smith, Wright.
Sub: Miller.
Scorers: Ipswich: Dixon (o.g.) 69; Arsenal: Wright 17, 40 (pen), 86, Youds (o.g.) 23, Parlour 51.
Referee: K Barrett (Coventry)
Attendance: 18,656

Ian Wright made an emphatic return from injury with a hat-trick three days after George Graham had judged him unfit to take his place against Torino. Wright, who had been forced out of the previous four matches with hamstring trouble, had been openly disappointed by Graham's decision.

Now against Ipswich all that pent-up frustration burst in a flood of goals.

Graham had made four changes in midfield and attack for the game, drafting in Wright, Ian Selley, Anders Limpar and Ray Parlour to replace Paul Merson, John Jensen, Paul Davis and Kevin Campbell. Yet they still went on to record their most emphatic League victory of the season.

"I wanted some fresh legs and the players who came in did well," said Graham. "Selley was outstanding. He has great potential and he's a born winner."

Wright, who had not scored since January, notched his first with a typical strike after 17 minutes when he received a pass from Lee Dixon and found the net with a fierce drive from an acute angle. Six minutes later Wright's pressure on Eddie Youds forced the Ipswich defender to turn Limpar's cross into his own net. And Wright was again at the centre of the action when he stepped up to convert a 40th-minute penalty after Mick Stockwell brought down Limpar. The ball was rifled into the top corner with angry arrogance.

Parlour added Arsenal's fourth in the 51st minute with a clever looping header over Clive Baker before Dixon presented Ipswich with the scant consolation of a headed own goal in the 69th minute.

With four minutes remaining Wright completed his hat-trick, slipping Tony Adams's pass beyond the advancing Baker. "We were outclassed," admitted Ipswich manager Mick McGiven.

Wright was quick to emphasise that any difference of opinion he had had with Graham was long gone. "As a professional I wasn't happy that I didn't play in Italy," he said. "But I'm just a player like any other in the team and I have to live with it. I'm 100 per cent behind the boss and it's entirely up to him to make the decisions."

Graham praised Wright but still found enough evidence to back his European decision. "His finishing was clinical and it was an

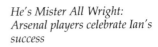

*He's Mister All Wright:
Arsenal players celebrate Ian's
success*

excellent display," he said. "But he was puffing in the last 20 minutes and he's still not fully fit. That's why he didn't play in Turin."

League Table After Match

	P	W	D	L	F	A	Pts
Man Utd.	30	20	8	2	59	28	68
Blackburn	31	19	7	5	46	23	64
Arsenal	31	14	12	5	39	17	54
Newcastle	30	15	6	9	52	30	51
Leeds.	30	12	12	6	42	30	48
Liverpool	31	13	8	10	49	42	47
Aston Villa	29	12	10	7	37	28	46
Sheffield Wed	30	11	11	8	53	39	44
Norwich	31	10	14	7	50	42	44
QPR	28	11	7	10	43	37	40
Wimbledon	29	10	9	10	34	40	39
Coventry	31	9	11	11	32	37	38
West Ham	30	9	11	10	28	38	38
Everton	31	10	6	15	35	42	36
Ipswich	30	8	12	10	27	37	36
Tottenham	32	7	11	14	32	46	32
Chelsea	29	8	8	13	31	39	32
Southampton	30	9	4	17	32	41	31
Man City	31	6	12	13	26	39	30
Oldham	30	6	9	15	26	50	27
Sheffield Utd.	30	4	12	14	26	47	24
Swindon	32	4	12	16	36	73	24

March 15

ARSENAL 1

TORINO 0
(Half-time score: 0-0)
(Arsenal won 1-0 on aggregate)

Arsenal: Seaman, Dixon, Winterburn, Davis, Bould, Adams, Jensen (Keown), Wright, Smith, Merson, Hillier (Selley).
Subs: Miller, Campbell, Limpar.
Torino: Galli, Annoni, Mussi, Cois, Gregucci, Fusi, Sinigaglia, Fortunato, Silenzi, Francescoli, Venturin.
Subs: Poggi, Jorni, Postine, Delii, Carri, Sottill.
Sent off: Torino: Gregucci.
Bookings: Arsenal: Selley (foul); Torino: Fortunato (foul).
Scorer: Arsenal: Adams 66.
Referee: J Blackenstein (Holland)
Attendance: 34,678

QUARTER FINAL, SECOND LEG

Tony Adams proved himself worthy to join Highbury's Hall of Fame with an outstanding personal performance. It was not only that he scored the match-winning goal – a trademark header full of commitment – but the way in which he stood firm against the worst of a growing Italian cynicism.

George Graham rightly hailed the result as a triumph for patience and discipline against an Italian team which came with the clinical purpose of heavy containment and swift counter-attack around the speeding Enzo Francescoli.

But, however sharp the Francescoli rapier, there was always Adams waiting to parry the thrust and show why Terry Venables had thought long and hard about making him England captain in his opening match against Denmark the previous week. Alongside Adams, Steve Bould was only marginally less imposing and Torino's frustration at facing them bubbled to the surface with a series of fouls.

Clearly Arsenal had learnt the bitter lessons of their Highbury defeat when they were caught by the pace of Benfica two seasons earlier. They presented a variety of play which pulled the Italians out of their defensive formation. If Ian Wright and Alan Smith found themselves shackled, Paul Merson had freedom elsewhere.

The platform was built by Arsenal's combative midfield. They lost David Hillier early with a serious ankle injury that needed eight stitches but Ian Selley came on to offer a spirit that was every inch as competitive.

John Jensen earned a standing ovation from the 34,678 Highbury crowd for his contribution when he was replaced late in the game. The creativity was left to Paul Davis and it was he who supplied the 66th-minute free-kick that led to Adams's goal.

David Seaman did not have a save to make all evening in contrast to Giovanni Galli who was called into urgent action as early as the 10th minute to save a Bould header from another Davis free-kick.

Andriea Silenzi raked his studs across Hillier's ankles after 16 minutes and Selley was so quickly into the heat of battle that he was cautioned within five minutes of coming on for a foul on Daniele

Fortunato who was in turn booked for hacking down Merson.

Angelo Gregucci followed him into the notebook of Dutch referee John Blankenstein for a foul on Wright. It was to prove costly two minutes from time when he repeated the action and was sent off.

Arsenal were equally reliable in the second half, coming under threat only from a misguided back-pass from Bould. Then, in the 66th minute, the game was won and Arsenal were through. Davis floated a free-kick which drifted tantalisingly away from Galli and there was Adams to complete his captain's role by heading home.

Graham was full of praise for Adams. "I always said that Frank McLintock was the best Arsenal skipper," said Graham, "but Tony has more silverware than him. Tony is a winner and tonight he was superb."

Adams celebrates his winner

March 19

SOUTHAMPTON 0

ARSENAL 4
(Half-time score: 0-2)

Southampton: Beasant, Kenna, Wood, Monkou, Charlton, Benali, Magilton, Dowie, Le Tissier, Maddison, Maskell.
Subs: Allen, Banger, Andrews.
Arsenal: Seaman, Dixon, Winterburn, Keown, Linighan, Adams, Campbell, Wright, Limpar (Smith), Selley, Parlour.
Subs: Morrow, Miller.
Bookings: Southampton: Monkou (foul), Allen (foul); Arsenal: Limpar (foul).
Scorers: Arsenal: Wright 18, 30, (pen) 68, Campbell 84.
Referee: D Frampton (Poole)
Attendance: 16,790

George Graham once again took the meat cleaver to his team, axing six men from the side which had beaten Torino the previous week. But once again the drastic tactic worked, with Ian Wright completing his second hat-trick in two weeks.

Out went Steve Bould, Paul Davis, John Jensen, Alan Smith, Paul Merson and David Hillier. In came Martin Keown – to shut out Matt Le Tissier – Andy Linighan, Kevin Campbell, Anders Limpar, Ian Selley and Ray Parlour. And Southampton were simply overwhelmed.

Wright took his tally for the season to 30 but was blamed by perfectionist Graham for failing to make the most of a late free-kick when Arsenal were already 4-0 up.

Southampton, under former Arsenal star Alan Ball, competed with Arsenal in most departments except for goalscoring. David Seaman made three outstanding saves while Dave Beasant at the other end was beaten four times but otherwise did not have a save to make.

Seaman kept out shots from Jeff Kenna and Craig Maskell and a close-range header from Neil Maddison in immaculate style.

By then Wright had given examples of his lethal goalscoring

That's unstoppable: Ian Wright takes off to head in the first of his hat-trick.

powers to put Arsenal firmly in control. His first came in the 18th minute when he dived to convert a centre fom Ian Selley. His second, a powerful volley on the half-hour, was even more impressive.

Southampton battled hard to bridge the gap in class but were finally undone in the 68th minute when Ken Monkou ended Limpar's dash from the halfway line with a foul in the area. Wright completed his hat-trick from the spot and Campbell was rewarded for an afternoon's honest toil with the fourth from close range six minutes from the end.

"Wright may be taking the ball home but he had only three kicks all day," said Ball. "Mind you, his first two goals were fantastic."

Graham explained his decision to leave out so many of his European heroes: "After the Torino match some of the players might have felt coming to Southampton was just another game. I wanted the fringe players to have the opportunity of showing what they could do. We did the same against Ipswich and it has worked well both times."

"We have many big games coming up and they all want to play in them. It's a great position for me."

League Table After Match

	P	W	D	L	F	A	Pts
Man Utd.	32	21	9	2	66	30	72
Blackburn	31	19	7	5	46	23	64
Newcastle	32	17	6	9	63	33	57
Arsenal	32	15	12	5	43	17	57
Leeds.	33	14	13	6	47	32	55
Liverpool	33	15	8	10	53	44	53
Aston Villa	33	13	10	10	39	33	49
QPR	31	13	8	10	49	41	47
Sheffield Wed	32	11	12	9	54	45	45
Norwich	32	10	14	8	53	46	44
Wimbledon	32	11	9	12	35	43	42
Ipswich	32	9	13	10	29	38	40
Coventry	33	9	11	13	32	39	38
West Ham	31	9	11	11	30	42	38
Everton	32	10	6	16	36	44	36
Chelsea	31	9	8	14	34	41	35
Tottenham	33	7	12	14	43	47	33
Southampton	32	9	5	18	33	46	32
Man City	33	6	13	14	26	40	30
Oldham	31	7	9	15	28	51	30
Sheffield Utd.	33	4	15	14	29	50	27
Swindon	34	4	13	17	39	82	25

March 22

ARSENAL **2**

MANCHESTER UNITED **2**
(Half-time score: 1-1)

Arsenal: Seaman, Dixon, Bould, Adams, Winterburn, Jensen, Selley, Davis (Campbell), Merson, Smith, Wright.
Subs: Keown, Miller.
Man Utd: Schmeichel, Parker, Pallister, Bruce, Irwin, Sharpe, Keane, Ince, Giggs, Hughes, Cantona.
Subs: Robson, Sealey, McClair.
Sent off: Man Utd: Cantona.
Bookings: Arsenal: Merson (foul); Man Utd: Keane (foul).
Scorers: Arsenal: Pallister (o.g) 36, Merson 78; Man Utd: Sharpe 10, 53.
Referee: V Callow (Solihull)
Attendance: 36,203

This was football's equivalent of the irresistible force meeting the unmovable object: Manchester United, the most prolific goalscorers in the Premier League, against Arsenal, the meanest defence in the country.

It was obvious something had to give...and in the end it was Eric Cantona, sent off for the second time in three days for two bookable offences. United players swarmed round referee Vic Callow to snarl their protests; the Frenchman strode straight towards the dug-out where manager Alex Ferguson offered a sympathetic hand.

The arguments about Cantona's dismissal were to rage for days. There was no doubt he had deserved to be booked for his first offence, a clattering tackle on Ian Selley. Some felt he could have been sent off for that. But opinion was divided about his second caution, when he appeared to be jumping away from Tony Adams rather than at him.

Roy Keane was also booked in an explosive match which contained passages of riveting football. There may be mutual respect between fellow Scots Ferguson and George Graham, but the goodwill does not seem to extend to the players.

United, at this stage still chasing their dream Treble, had come to win and, with Andrei Kanchelskis injured, drafted in Lee Sharpe for his return after a hernia operation. He was to prove their hero.

Arsenal had not set out their stall to be onlookers. Competition in midfield was almost on a war footing between Paul Ince and Roy Keane for United and Ian Selley and John Jensen for Arsenal.

The early sparrings ended in sensational fashion. David Seaman's normally safe hands spilled a Mark Hughes drive in the 10th minute and Sharpe, alert and decisive, was on hand to slam the ball into the net.

United survived a triple assault on their goal midway through the half. Peter Schmeichel blocked a shot from Ian Wright, Steve Bruce stopped another from Alan Smith and Ince cleared off the line from Paul Davis.

But in the 36th minute Arsenal were level from a fortunate free-kick. Bruce was judged by a linesman to have handled the ball when it struck his shoulder. Merson swung over the free-kick and, as Schmeichel stayed on his line, the ball skimmed into the net off Gary Pallister's shin.

United were back in front after 53 minutes. Ryan Giggs found Cantona on the left, took the return ball and his shot screwed fortunately off Winterburn to Sharpe, who stroked home his second.

When Schmeichel saved twice at the feet of Wright it looked as if United would secure the victory they needed to ease their position at the top of the table. But then Lee Dixon lifted the ball over a square United defence and, as Denis Irwin seemed to be impeded by the referee, Paul Merson took the ball on and drove it fiercely in off the inside of the far post.

Nerve-ends were exposed and Cantona argued his case in vain when he made his two-footed tackle on Selley. Two minutes later he lunged at Adams and off he went.

Below, left: Adams looks on as Cantona is booked

League Table After Match

	P	W	D	L	F	A	Pts
Man Utd.	33	21	10	2	68	32	73
Blackburn	32	20	7	5	54	24	67
Newcastle	33	18	6	9	65	33	60
Arsenal	33	15	13	5	47	19	58
Leeds	33	14	13	6	47	32	55
Liverpool	33	15	8	10	53	44	53
Aston Villa	33	13	10	10	39	33	49
Norwich	33	11	14	8	56	46	47
QPR	31	13	8	10	49	41	47
Sheffield Wed	33	11	12	10	55	47	45
Wimbledon	32	11	9	12	35	43	42
Ipswich	33	9	13	11	29	40	40
Coventry	33	9	11	13	32	39	38
West Ham	31	9	11	11	30	42	38
Everton	33	10	6	17	36	47	36
Chelsea	31	9	8	14	34	41	35
Tottenham	33	7	12	14	43	47	33
Southampton	32	9	5	18	33	46	32
Man City	33	6	13	14	26	40	31
Oldham	31	7	9	15	28	51	30
Sheffield Utd	33	4	15	14	29	50	29
Swindon	34	4	13	17	39	82	25

March 26

ARSENAL 1

LIVERPOOL 0
(Half-time score: 0-0)

Arsenal: Seaman, Dixon, Keown, Parlour, Bould, Linighan, Jensen (Morrow), Wright (Smith), Campbell, Merson, Selley.
Sub: Miller.
Liverpool: James, Jones, Dicks, Wright, Ruddock, Redknapp, McManaman, Whelan, Rush, Fowler, Barnes.
Subs: Nicol, Thomas, Grobbelaar.
Scorer: Arsenal: Merson 47.
Referee: R Hart (Darlington)
Attendance: 35,556

Paul Merson would probably have put it in more colourful language had George Graham not been sitting beside him. He had been asked how Arsenal players felt about being victims of a squad system in which few were ever sure of selection.

"The boss picks the team," he said diplomatically. "If you are not in it, you are not in it." He might have added: "It's no good knocking on this fellow's door."

Graham's willingness to exile dissenters to the reserves rather than grant lucrative transfers is well known. But Merson expressed positive reasons for his periodic omission. "This is a big club. Everyone understands that if you are not here the chances are you'll be at a smaller, less successful club. I wasn't in the sides that played Southampton and Ipswich recently. The lads were brilliant. Not many teams get changed after hitting five and four goals away from home."

Graham may hardly fit the image of a true gambler, yet no one seems to have shuffled a pack better in the season. As he put it: "The inconsistency of selection has produced consistency of results."

He dealt another hand against Liverpool and, although they nearly called his bluff, it proved to be a winner, thanks to Merson's 47th-minute strike.

Merson, who has presented Graham with a few off-the-field headaches over the years, was at his exciting best against Liverpool, a club whose squad system Graham had always tried to emulate.

And, to Graham's credit Merson appeared to have reacted positively to being left in the wilderness earlier this season. "I have worked hard," said Merson. "And I feel really good at the moment. I go running on my own at the end of training now when I'm not playing. Even at this stage of the season I think you have to keep ticking over."

For a second he allowed his natural humour to surface when he added: "I don't do it when the boss is around because you can stop when you're on your own."

Merson must have impressed the watching England coach Terry Venables as well as the Paris St Germain coach Artur Jorge who was repaying the visit Graham had made to his club the previous night.

With the match against Paris St Germain in the European Cup Winners' Cup semi-final looming three days later, Graham decided

Merson scores the winner

to rest captain Tony Adams together with Nigel Winterburn and Paul Davis.

Merson's goal, after fine work from Ray Parlour and a final pass by Ian Selley, was poor reward on an afternoon of haphazard finishing. Merson, twice, Kevin Campbell and Parlour all wasted first-half chances.

Merson headed wide and David James saved superbly from Campbell before the pattern of the game changed and cast doubts on Graham's gamble.

The substitution of John Jensen, a tireless worker in front of defence, and the switching of Steve McManaman from right to left appeared to contribute to Liverpool's eventual domination of the last 20 minutes.

While goalkeeper David Seaman deserved praise for his agility and alertness in saving on each occasion, Jamie Redknapp, Ian Rush and McManaman should all have scored in the closing stages.

Liverpool boss Roy Evans admitted later that his side was lacking self-belief. "It took Arsenal to score before we started to play any progressive football," he said. "Then we thought there was nothing to lose and had decent chances.

"It's a matter of belief. We should have been playing like that from the start."

League Table After Match

	P	W	D	L	F	A	Pts
Man Utd.	34	22	10	2	69	32	76
Blackburn	34	21	7	6	52	29	70
Newcastle	34	19	6	9	68	33	63
Arsenal	34	16	13	5	46	19	61
Leeds	34	14	13	7	47	33	55
Liverpool	35	15	8	12	53	46	53
QPR	32	14	8	10	52	42	50
Aston Villa	34	13	11	10	39	33	50
Sheffield Wed	34	12	12	10	58	48	48
Wimbledon	34	13	9	12	40	44	48
Norwich	35	11	14	10	57	51	47
Coventry	34	10	11	13	34	40	41
Ipswich	35	9	14	12	32	45	41
Chelsea	33	10	8	15	37	44	38
West Ham	33	9	11	13	32	47	38
Everton	35	10	7	18	36	48	37
Tottenham	34	8	12	14	44	47	36
Oldham	33	8	10	15	31	52	34
Man City	35	6	15	14	28	42	33
Southampton	34	9	6	19	34	49	33
Sheffield Utd.	35	5	16	14	32	52	31
Swindon	35	4	13	18	40	85	25

March 29

PARIS ST GERMAIN 1

ARSENAL 1
(Half-time score: 0-1)

Paris St Germain: Lama, Llacer, Colleter, Ricardo, Sassos, Le Guen, Fournier, Guerin, Weah, Valdo, Ginola.
Subs: Bravo, Cobos, Kombouare, Gravelaine, Borrelli.
Arsenal: Seaman, Dixon, Winterburn, Davis (Keown), Bould, Adams, Jensen, Wright, Smith (Campbell), Merson, Sealey.
Subs: Morrow, Miller, McGoldrick.
Bookings: Arsenal: Adams (foul), Merson (foul).
Scorers: Paris St Germain: Ginola 50; Arsenal: Wright 35.
Referee: L Sundell (Sweden)
Attendance: 46,000

SEMI-FINAL, FIRST LEG

Ian Wright had expected to spend a frustrating night in Paris sitting on the substitutes' bench. Instead he used his head to give Arsenal the lift they needed in the first leg of their European Cup Winners' Cup semi-final with only the sixth goal conceded by Paris St Germain at the Parc des Princes all season.

George Graham's capacity to evaluate the demands of his European campaign had tended to be accurate all season and this time his decision to play Wright from the start proved the correct move once again.

Wright's glancing header from a fine Paul Davis free-kick provided the precious away score and had Arsenal looking optimistically ahead to the return leg in two weeks.

Graham said: "I hope the referee in London will be as generous to the home team as he was here. But David Seaman hardly had a shot to save and we were very motivated."

Arsenal showed true professionalism in this performance against the sophisticated French side who had gone 35 matches without defeat. They showed commendable discipline and huge patience as they set about creating their opportunities. Above all their fitness and relentless strength sapped the French.

John Jensen was a worthy man of the match thanks to his unselfish industry. His contribution was as significant as Wright's.

The French had quick, inventive forwards, yet they were rendered almost sterile by the excellence of Arsenal's back four, even if it did cost Tony Adams a caution.

Adams was a commanding figure, assisted by Nigel Winterburn, whose second-half goal-line clearance proved crucial. Graham was frustrated that his defence was beaten at the near post for the French equaliser in the second half. But that only emphasised the perfectionist in him, and there were many heroes. Young Ian Selley tackled relentlessly, Davis probed intelligently and Paul Merson showed the danger of his pace.

The adventure began to unfold midway through the first half after some early sparring. It needed a quality save from goalkeeper Bernard Lama to keep out a Jensen shot following a five-man move and the effort seemed to ignite the Arsenal fuse.

They exploded shortly afterwards when Alan Smith was brought down by Brazilian Ricardo Gomes just outside the penalty area. Smith took the free-kick and Wright was on to the ball at speed, glancing a precision header past Lama. It was a devastating strike and Wright darted to the Arsenal bench to receive the acclaim he deserved.

The half was marred only by the caution of Adams for the second of two heavy challenges on French Footballer of the Year David Ginola.

The dangerous and elusive striker brought consolation for PSG early in the second half. A corner on the left was curled into the near post by Brazilian Valdo Candido and Ginola got in the finest of touches with his head to score the equalising goal.

Arsenal might still have emerged as winners. A lovely pass from Jensen freed Merson. As he cut inside and was tackled the ball broke perfectly for Smith who, despite the smothering challenge of Lana, really should have scored.

April 2

ARSENAL 1

SWINDON 1
(Half-time score: 1-1)

Arsenal: Seaman, Dixon, Keown, Davis, Linighan, Adams, Jensen (McGoldrick), Wright, Smith, Merson (Campbell), Parlour.
Sub: Miller.
Swindon: Hammond, Summerbee, Bodin, Nijholt, Taylor, Whitbread, Kilcline, Moncur, Scott, Fjortoft, Sanchez.
Subs: Horlock, McAvennie, Digby.
Booking: Swindon: Nijholt (foul).
Scorers: Arsenal: Smith 4; Swindon: Bodin (pen) 29.
Referee: B Hill (Kettering)
Attendance: 31,634

George Graham refused to make excuses after his European heroes were booed off following the drab draw with Swindon.

"We started brightly, then got sloppy," said the Arsenal boss. "We were coasting at times but their goal lifted them, and the crowd got a bit frustrated. "These days they cheer when we win and they boo when we lose. It is sad but all part of modern living."

Graham shuffled his pack again but could not come up with a winning hand. The Arsenal manager made three changes from the side that drew in the European Cup Winners' Cup in Paris but found the Premiership bottom club in no mood to lie down.

Not even a dream start with a goal inside five minutes could inspire the Gunners and Graham added: "It was just a matter of breaking them down. We had most of the play but to their credit Swindon defended well. They had a good result against Manchester United recently and drew away at Liverpool and have shown that they are capable of getting a result.

"But I'm disappointed and, if we had scored another, it might have been four or five. The penalty lifted them and the crowd became frustrated,"

Swindon went behind when Ray Parlour set up Alan Smith for the simplest of goals. Smith's header from a yard out was the 86th Premiership goal Swindon had conceded and a drubbing on a scale of the St James' Park massacre three weeks before looked on the cards.

But it was Arsenal goalkeeper David Seaman who was picking the ball out of the net next. On a rare sortie into Arsenal territory John Moncur broke down the left and was hauled down in the box by Paul Davis.

Referee Brian Hill, standing in for the injured Keith Hackett, pointed to the spot and Paul Bodin hit an unstoppable penalty into the roof of the net.

Graham could hardly contain his anger. Perhaps the three changes he made from the European match should have been 11.

His presence in the dug-out at the start of the second half failed to ignite his lacklustre side, who might have fallen behind twice in the opening quarter-hour. Only an inspired intervention by Andy

Linighan denied Keith Scott and minutes later Tony Adams brilliantly intercepted Jan Fjortoft.

Indeed it was the visitors who finished the stronger and, but for some desperate Arsenal defending, Swindon might have pulled off a coveted first away victory in the Premiership.

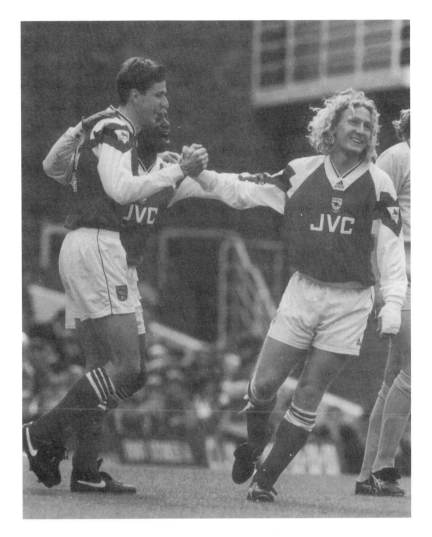

Double Act: Smith and Parlour celebrate their goal

League Table After Match

	P	W	D	L	F	A	Pts
Man Utd.	35	22	10	3	69	34	76
Blackburn	35	22	7	6	54	29	73
Newcastle	35	19	7	9	69	34	64
Arsenal	35	16	14	5	47	20	62
Leeds	35	14	14	7	48	34	56
Liverpool	36	15	8	13	54	48	53
Sheffield Wed	35	13	12	10	63	49	51
Wimbledon	35	14	9	12	42	45	51
QPR	33	14	8	11	53	46	50
Aston Villa	35	13	11	11	39	36	50
Norwich	36	11	14	11	58	53	47
Chelsea	34	11	8	15	39	44	41
Coventry	35	10	11	14	35	42	41
West Ham	34	10	11	13	34	48	41
Ipswich	36	9	14	13	33	47	41
Tottenham	35	9	12	14	46	48	39
Everton	36	10	7	19	37	53	37
Oldham	34	9	10	15	35	43	37
Man City	36	7	15	14	31	42	36
Sheffield Utd	36	6	16	14	34	53	34
Southampton	35	9	6	20	34	51	33
Swindon	36	4	14	18	41	86	26

April 4

SHEFFIELD UNITED 1

ARSENAL 1
(Half-time score: 0-0)

Sheff Utd: Tracey, Nilsen, Beesley, Tuttle, Bradshaw, Gannon, Rogers, Whitehouse, Hodges, Littlejohn, Flo.
Subs: Hartfield, Blake, Bibb.
Arsenal: Seaman, Keown (Dixon), Adams, Bould, Winterburn, Selley, Parlour, Campbell, McGoldrick (Merson), Smith, Wright.
Sub: Miller.
Booking: Sheffield United: Whitehouse (foul).
Scorers: Sheffield United: Rogers 54; Arsenal: Campbell 69.
Referee: D Frampton (Poole)
Attendance: 20,019

Dave Bassett rewarded his battling Sheffield United side with a two-day golfing holiday at The Belfry after they earned another vital point in their annual flirtation with the drop.

It was a thoroughly deserved point for the Blades, although Arsenal appeared to be playing on auto-pilot for much of the game, full of effort and commitment but lacking the inspiration needed to trouble a resilient Sheffield side.

And their usually rock-solid defence survived a number of scares in the first half as the speedy Adrian Littlejohn gave Tony Adams and Co the run-around.

Twice England goalkeeper David Seaman had to race off his line to save bravely at the feet of Littlejohn and he was lucky to see a Glyn Hodges shot fly just wide of the post.

The home side, with two vital wins in the past week, finally went ahead in the 54th minute thanks to a traditional Bassett tactic – the long throw to the near post.

Norwegian defender Roger Nilsen launched the missile into the box, compatriot Jostein Flo missed his header but Paul Rogers made no mistake with the touch into goal past Seaman.

The home crowd went wild with dreams of a victory to lift them out of the bottom three and a first League win against the Gunners since 1973.

But the goal stirred Arsenal to concentrate their minds on attack. Within a minute Ian Selley headed against the post from a cross by Eddie McGoldrick.

Ian Wright headed straight at home keeper Simon Tracey from another curling McGoldrick cross and the almost inevitable equaliser came in the 69th minute. Again it was McGoldrick who provided the service and this time Kevin Campbell's back-flick flew past the stranded Tracey to extend Arsenal's unbeaten run to 14 games.

It was tough luck on the hugely impressive David Tuttle, who played a starring role at the heart of the United defence, snuffing out the threat of Wright.

His £350,000 signing from Spurs last summer looked a bargain, especially as Bassett's men attempted another great escape.

My safe hands: David Seaman produces two brave saves cannot stop Nilsen's missile

Bassett was happy with the draw, knowing there will be no tougher opposition against which to score. "I can't complain with us getting four points over Easter against Arsenal and Liverpool," he said. "Maybe we'll look back on this game as a vital draw.

"It's still wide open at the bottom and we just have to win as many games as possible and hope that others are dragged down to where we are now."

League Table After Match

	P	W	D	L	F	A	Pts
Man Utd.	36	23	10	3	72	36	79
Blackburn	36	23	7	6	57	29	76
Newcastle	36	19	8	9	69	34	65
Arsenal	36	16	15	5	48	21	63
Leeds.	36	15	14	7	52	34	59
Sheffield Wed	36	14	12	10	64	49	54
Liverpool	37	15	9	13	55	49	54
Wimbledon	36	14	10	12	43	46	52
Aston Villa	36	13	12	11	39	36	51
QPR	34	14	8	12	53	50	50
Norwich	37	11	15	11	58	53	48
Coventry	36	11	11	14	37	42	44
West Ham	35	11	11	13	38	49	44
Chelsea	35	11	9	15	39	44	42
Ipswich	37	9	14	14	33	49	41
Tottenham	36	9	12	15	47	52	39
Man City	37	8	15	14	32	42	39
Everton	37	10	7	20	37	56	37
Oldham	35	9	10	16	37	56	37
Sheffield Utd.	37	6	17	14	35	54	35
Southampton	36	9	6	21	34	52	33
Swindon	37	4	14	19	41	87	26

April 12

ARSENAL 1

PARIS ST GERMAIN 0
(Half-time score 2-0)
(Arsenal won 2-1 on aggregate)

Arsenal: Seaman; Dixon, Winterburn (Keown), Davis (Hillier), Bould, Adams, Jensen, Wright, Smith, Campbell, Selley.
Subs: Miller, McGoldrick, Parlour.
Paris SG: Lama; Sassus, Colleter, Ricardo, Roche, Le-Guen, Fournier, Guerin, Rai, Valdo, Ginola.
Subs: Llacer, Kombouare, Grauelaine, Cobos, Borrelli.
Bookings: Arsenal: Wright (foul); Paris SG: Colletes (foul), Ricardo (foul).
Referee: P Mikkelsen (Denmark)
Attendance: 34,212

SEMI-FINAL, SECOND LEG

Celebrations were tinged with tears as Arsenal made it to a Cup Winners' Cup final in Copenhagen on May 4.

Kevin Campbell's fifth-minute goal at an emotionally charged Highbury was the forerunner to a desperate defensive display as Arsenal clawed their way defiantly to Denmark. But the booking that put Wright out of the final brought the night its real drama.

A needless, headstrong tackle by 32-goal striker Wright five minutes from half-time was like putting a pistol to his own temple and pulling the trigger. And he knew it. He sank to his knees and buried his head in his hands. And sure enough, when he looked up, Peter Mikkelsen was brandishing the yellow card.

He was inconsolable and the tears flowed. The clouds, which dispensed a steady drizzle on North London, might have been weeping for him too. At the age of 30, Wright may not have many finals left for him. But five Arsenal players had gone into the game with the threat of suspension hanging over them and none of the others allowed his discipline to lapse.

Though that undoubtedly took the edge off the evening, sympathy should not submerge the elation that English football can take from a marvellous achievement.

Arsenal were facing one of the slickest sides in Europe, who had lost once in their previous 39 matches and galloping away with the French Championship. They had plenty of savoir-faire and a good deal of skill to go with it, inspired by the samba soccer of their three Brazilian internationals. The greasy conditions served only to benefit their rotating, short-passing game.

In Valdo they had a player in the true Brazilian tradition and he hardly deserved to finish on the losing side, though his impact was diminished by the close attention John Jensen.

If the sympathy goes to Wright, if the goal goes to Campbell, then the medals should go first to the men at the back of the Arsenal team, who perhaps do not always get the credit their organisation deserves. They were primed superbly for combat by George Graham and they took all the considerable and varied artillery thrown at them by the French.

For Henry V at Agincourt read Tony Adams at Highbury. He had his band of brothers prepared to shed blood with him, too, in Steve Bould and Lee Dixon as well as Nigel Winterburn, carried stretcher from the action late in the game.

Theirs was an heroic defiance with Adams leading not only by example but with a constant dialogue of exhortation and cajoling, applauding the good and castigating the bad.

Those admonishments were often directed at his midfield and were harsh on occasions, too, for Jensen and Ian Selley worked to the edge of exhaustion to try to break the fluency of the French.

It was a relentless and sapping cup tie, always in the balance, always fiercely competitive and never without its suspense right from the opening minutes when David Seaman almost gifted St Germain a goal.

As he tried to bowl the greasy ball out it slewed from his hand straight to the fleet feet of Valdo, and it needed one of those octopus lunges from Adams on Rai to deny the French a flying start.

But the game was only five minutes into its exciting course when Arsenal scored, a neat move with Alan Smith feeding Dixon's overlap on the right. Bernard Lama was in two minds whether to come for it but the ball dropped short and the merest flick from Campbell's broad forehead was enough to steer it inside the near post.

The French, who had described Arsenal as slobs and louts in pre-match verbal sparring, were no sophisticates themselves on occasions and Patrick Colleter was cautioned for felling the combative Jensen.

Ricardo might have headed the French level from Valdo's corner and Rai, brother of the famous Socrates, steered another corner off target as Arsenal lived dangerously.

Then, as the temperature rose on the pitch, Ricardo collected a yellow card for a challenge on Campbell. It should have been a warning to Wright, who lost his final chance two minutes later by charging into Alain Roche when there was no danger and little chance of winning the ball.

It was a backs-to-the-wall effort in the second half, though Wright recovered his composure to attempt a couple of off-target shots.

David Ginola, France's Player of the Year, ought to have carried the game towards extra time in the 72nd minute but he blazed the chance wide when allowed an opening by an isolated defensive lapse.

Graham closed ranks, David Hillier replacing the tiring Paul Davis to tighten up the defences, and the move worked admirably. By now Adams was in control, a majestic man, standing tall as players around him wilted through sheer physical effort.

April 16

ARSENAL 1

CHELSEA 0
(Half-time score: 0-0)

Arsenal: Seaman, Dixon, Keown, Adams, Morrow, Parlour, Hillier (Smith), Selley, McGoldrick, Wright, Campbell.
Subs: Linighan, Miller.
Chelsea: Kharine, Clarke, Kjeldberg, Lee, Sinclair, Donaghy, Wise, Hopkins, Newton, Spencer, Peacock.
Subs: Barnard, Spackman, Hitchcock.
Booking: Arsenal: Keown (foul).
Scorer: Arsenal: Wright 72.
Referee: A Wilkie (Chester-Le-Street)
Attendance: 34,314

League Table After Match

	P	W	D	L	F	A	Pts
Man Utd.	37	23	10	4	72	37	79
Blackburn	38	24	7	7	59	32	79
Newcastle	38	20	8	10	72	36	68
Arsenal	37	17	15	5	49	21	66
Leeds.	36	15	14	7	52	34	59
Sheffield Wed	38	15	13	10	68	51	58
Liverpool	39	16	9	14	56	51	57
Wimbledon	37	15	10	12	44	46	55
Aston Villa	38	14	12	12	41	38	54
QPR	37	15	9	13	57	55	54
Norwich	39	11	16	12	63	59	49
Coventry	38	12	12	14	39	43	48
West Ham	37	12	11	14	40	51	47
Chelsea	37	11	10	16	40	46	43
Man City	39	9	16	14	35	44	43
Ipswich	39	9	15	15	34	51	42
Everton	39	11	7	21	39	58	40
Tottenham	37	9	12	16	47	53	39
Southampton	38	11	6	21	42	57	39
Oldham	36	9	10	17	38	58	37
Sheffield Utd.	38	6	17	15	36	56	35
Swindon	38	4	15	19	42	88	27

Kevin Campbell seemed to have been in the shadow of his friend and Arsenal striking partner Ian Wright for much of the season. When Campbell scored a hat-trick at Swindon in December, Wright stole the headlines with an outrageous last-minute wonder goal.

When Campbell's header put Arsenal into the European Cup Winners' Cup final, Wright again commanded centre stage when he cried buckets at getting foolishly booked.

In this match, despite Campbell's authoritative display at centre-forward, Wright scored the only goal and was all over Highbury's big TV screen singing the club's new and appropriate ditty 'One-nil to the Arsenal'.

But Wright would not be available for the battle in Copenhagen against Parma the following month and George Graham knew he must preserve the form and sometimes brittle self-belief of Campbell until then.

The Gunners' manager said: "Kevin was the outstanding player on the pitch, he was tremendous. I've told him that we all have great confidence in his ability. "He's got 19 goals this season, which puts him in the top six strikers in the country. I think he is an excellent player and we hope Copenhagen will be his stage."

That assessment was a little flattering. Campbell had scored 14 goals in the season, the measure continental football uses, and that puts him 11th in the English list.

Graham also called this game "very exciting", whereas Chelsea boss Glenn Hoddle's verdict was "not a wonderful match to the eye".

But Graham is a keen student of history and knows that Nelson (Horatio, not Sammy) won the original battle of Copenhagen because he deliberately did not see the whole picture and ignored warning signs.

Chelsea had their minds very much on the approaching FA Cup final and, with six players injured, it was not a match to assess their prospects.

But Hoddle's decision to play David Lee at sweeper, using that preferred tactic for the first time in months, perhaps revealed that he will return to it for his Chelsea revolution in the long-term. Graham was most admiring, saying: "It was an interesting tactical battle and Chelsea were very hard to break down."

April 19

A rare goal from Steve Bould maintained Arsenal's unbeaten run but the main gossip of a largely uneventful night was that Eddie McGoldrick, Arsenal's £1.1 million midfielder, was set to return to Crystal Palace in the summer.

Republic of Ireland international McGoldrick, a target of abuse from Highbury fans since joining the Gunners, was reportedly wanted by newly promoted Palace and, after the barracking he had received from a section of Arsenal fans during Saturday's match against Chelsea, he was expected to jump at the move.

McGoldrick was missing from this match, needed on international duty, as Arsenal escaped the fate of so many of Wimbledon's mighty opponents.

Joe Kinnear's Crazy Gang had deposited all the Premiership's top clubs on their backsides over the previous months and were in search of a nap-hand of scalps after wins against Manchester United, Blackburn, Newcastle and Leeds.

Arsenal's England goalkeeper Dave Seaman took the blame for Robbie Earle's 38th-minute goal, failing to cut out Gary Elkins' corner which Earle headed home at the far post. Stewart Castledine, a youngster replacing the injured Vinnie Jones, had already tested Seaman but, when Elkins crossed, the England goalkeeper was clutching air. Earle rose superbly at the far post to head home.

"Dave held up his hands at the end," said Graham. "There was too much pace on the cross but he made two great saves afterwards."

Bould equalised, slamming the ball home after Ian Selley's corner eluded a mass of bodies.

Arsenal were bidding for a European passport in case their Cup Winners' Cup final with Parma ended in defeat in May. They knew that overtaking third-placed Newcastle – if Blackburn won the title and Manchester United the FA Cup – would give them entry.

Yet Arsenal, undefeated in 15 League games since December, looked vulnerable to the well-organised Wimbledon outfit. John Fashanu and Dean Holdsworth might have ended up match-winners but Kevin Campbell and Lee Dixon, who hit the post, might have been heroes at the other end.

ARSENAL 1
WIMBLEDON 1
(Half-time score: 0-1)

Arsenal: Seaman, Dixon, Adams, Bould, Keown, Parlour, Davis (Flatts), Selley, Wright, Smith, Campbell.
Sub: Linighan, Miller.
Wimbledon: Segers, Barton, Scales, Blackwell, Elkins, Fear, Earle, Castledine, Goyle, Holdsworth, Pershaw.
Subs: Clarke, Perry, Sullivan.
Booking: Wimbledon: Scales (foul).
Scorers: Arsenal: Bould 51; Wimbledon: Earle 37.
Referee: G Gifford (Mid-Glam)
Attendance: 21,292

League Table After Match

	P	W	D	L	F	A	Pts
Man Utd.	37	23	10	4	72	37	79
Blackburn	38	24	7	7	59	32	79
Newcastle	38	20	8	10	72	36	68
Arsenal	38	17	16	5	50	22	67
Leeds	37	16	14	7	54	34	62
Sheffield Wed	38	15	13	10	68	51	58
Liverpool	39	16	9	14	56	51	57
Wimbledon	38	15	11	12	45	47	56
Aston Villa	38	14	12	12	41	38	54
QPR	37	15	9	13	57	55	54
Norwich	39	11	16	12	63	59	49
Coventry	38	12	12	14	39	43	48
West Ham	37	12	11	14	40	51	47
Chelsea	37	11	10	16	40	46	43
Man City	39	9	16	14	35	44	43
Ipswich	39	9	15	15	34	51	42
Everton	39	11	7	21	39	58	40
Tottenham	38	9	12	17	47	55	39
Southampton	38	11	6	21	42	57	39
Oldham	36	9	10	17	38	58	37
Sheffield Utd	38	6	17	15	36	56	35
Swindon	38	4	15	19	42	88	27

April 23

ASTON VILLA 1

ARSENAL 2
(Half-time score: 0-1)

Aston Villa: Spink, Barrett, Teale, Richardson, Houghton, Atkinson, Townsend, Ehiogu, Cox, Farrell, Fenton.
Subs: Oakes, Saunders, Beinlich.
Arsenal: Seaman, Dixon, Davis (Parlour), Linighan, Campbell, Wright, Smith, Bould, Keown, Morrow, Flatts.
Subs: Miller, McGoldrick.
Booking: Arsenal: Davis (dissent).
Scorers: Aston Villa: Houghton 57; Arsenal: Wright (pen) 30, 90.
Referee: K Cooper (Pontypridd)
Attendance: 31,580

Ian Wright left his exit late. The Arsenal coach was revving up and players were being urged to put down their pints of lager when he emerged on to the Villa steps, arms held high in triumph.

But he is a king without a crown. Suspension will keep him out of the European Cup Winners' Cup final – something 30,000 Villa fans kept reminding him .

"That wound me up," said Wright after his two goals had stretched Arsenal's unbeaten Premiership run to 18 games. " It's all it took," he said, signing autographs as he went. " I felt full of it. It backfired on Villa, didn't it?"

Villa's fans chanted: "Ian Wright, where's your final gone?" from the Holte End and it was picked up all over the ground, sending Wright into a frenzy of action and turning an end-of-season game into a personal crusade.

"I wanted to prove them wrong - know what I mean?" said Wright. "I'm choked about missing the final enough as it is, so I didn't need all that, did I? It showed 'em in the end. They got me going. I love that, when people have a go. It fired me up."

When Wright put away Arsenal's dodgy first-half penalty for an alleged foul by Neil Cox, he milked it for all it was worth, parading around with both arms held high longer than Michael Moorer after his shock win over Evander Holyfield.

He encouraged Arsenal fans behind the goal to drown out the sarcasm coming from the opposite end of the pitch and then, in the very last minute, had the final word. Kevin Campbell created the chance , opening up Villa's defence, and Wright finished cleanly, his 34th goal in 49 games this season.

If the watching Parma manager allowed himself a sigh of relief that Wright is out of the final, who could blame him?

"Of course we will miss him," Alan Smith said, who plays so well the straight man in the double act with Wright. "He was so bubbly, the Villa fans certainly got him going."

"Missing the final is a bad blow for Ian but we know he's not going to be around and we have to get on with it. There are enough good players at the club for us to overcome his suspension."

Ron Atkinson, who saw Wright deny Villa something from one

Ian Wright celebrates his second goal in the last minute of the game

of their better post-Coca-Cola Cup performances, reckons Arsenal would be certainties for the Cup Winners' Cup with him playing. Without him? "It makes things more difficult," said Atkinson, "but I still think Arsenal will do it, they are so resilient."

Only Bolton – when they were at the height of their FA Cup giant-killing – had beaten Arsenal since December 18 and their confidence showed even when Villa, inspired by new star Graham Fenton, equalised with a superb Ray Houghton lob over David Seaman.

Dalian Atkinson might have taken the win off the Gunners but Seaman stopped him twice, point-blank, and Shaun Teale, who tried to keep the lid on Wright all afternoon, said: "Anyone is bound to miss Ian Wright. He was bouncy and chatty all day but don't underestimate Arsenal without him. Alan Smith is stronger than he looks – almost impossible to win the ball off in the air – and Campbell is good.

"I hope they win the Cup Winners' Cup. It will be good for football in this country."

League Table After Match

	P	W	D	L	F	A	Pts
Man Utd.	38	24	10	4	74	37	82
Blackburn	38	24	7	7	59	32	79
Newcastle	39	21	8	10	75	38	71
Arsenal	39	18	16	5	52	23	70
Leeds	38	16	15	7	55	35	63
Sheffield Wed	39	16	13	10	73	51	61
Liverpool	40	17	9	14	58	52	60
Wimbledon	39	16	11	12	49	49	59
QPR	37	15	9	13	57	55	54
Aston Villa	39	14	12	13	42	40	54
Norwich	40	11	16	13	63	60	49
Coventry	39	12	13	14	39	43	49
West Ham	38	12	11	15	41	53	47
Chelsea	38	11	11	16	41	47	44
Man City	40	9	16	15	35	46	43
Tottenham	39	10	12	17	50	55	42
Ipswich	40	9	15	16	34	56	42
Everton	40	11	8	21	39	58	41
Southampton	39	11	6	22	42	60	39
Sheffield Utd	39	7	17	15	37	56	38
Oldham	37	9	10	18	40	61	37
Swindon	39	4	15	20	44	92	27

April 27

QPR 1

ARSENAL 1
(Half-time score: 1-0)

QPR: Roberts, Bardsley, Ready, Yates, Wilson, Holloway, Wilkins, Barker, Impey, White, Penrice.
Subs: Allen, Brevett, Stejskal.
Arsenal: Seaman, Dixon, Linighan, Adams, Keown (McGoldrick), Flatts (Selley), Parlour, Morrow, Merson, Wright, Smith.
Sub: Miller.
Scorers: QPR: Penrice 3; Arsenal: Merson 46.
Referee: I Borrett (Gt Yarmouth)
Attendance: 11,442

George Graham saw Martin Keown limp off with a hamstring injury and goalkeeper David Seaman suffer a knock to add to Arsenal's problems seven days before their Cup Winners' Cup final against Parma in Copenhagen.

Arsenal knew they would already be without suspended Ian Wright and crocked John Jensen for that match while Nigel Winterburn and David Hillier were both recovering from setbacks.

Yet Graham said after this thrilling draw: "If a player is injured out there, I do not immediately start thinking of next week. How can I? The adrenalin was flowing for this match, not another one. When Seaman went down I did not start thinking about Parma next week but about QPR tonight.

"I never worry about things you can't influence. But we are running out of players and we will just have to get on with it."

Keown, renowned for his man-to-man marking, played in seven of Arsenal's eight European ties but the England defender came off 17 minutes from time.

Seaman looked in deep trouble after needing five minutes of treatment when he was caught by Rangers' Bradley Allen as the striker chased a long ball. But the Arsenal goalkeeper played on, despite continually holding his right side, and produced two outstanding saves to suggest he was not as badly hurt as first feared.

"It was a high tackle on David," said Graham, "and he has some stud marks on his chest."

A London derby that has a reputation of failing to produce a goal defied recent history by conjuring up some cracking football.

But Rangers boss Gerry Francis was left angry as referee Ian Borrett turned down what appeared to be two clear QPR penalties.

Stephen Morrow seemed to bring down David Bardsley in the box and then minutes later Lee Dixon handled as the ball came towards him.

Francis said: "I might say Arsenal had a little bit of help out there. Let's just say I had a couple of words with the referee.

"I thought the first one was a definite penalty. But there is not much you can do. I'm not too pleased about it. There are so many issues concerning relegation and promotion that a lot of other

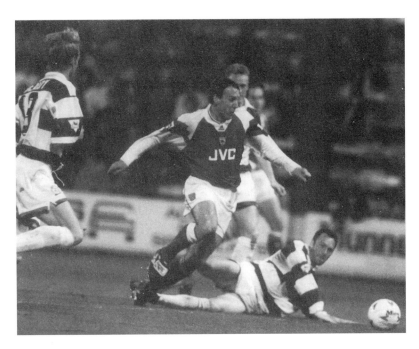

Merson runs through to score the equaliser for Arsenal

people and teams would have been disappointed with the decision. But I was pleased with our performance and I hope Arsenal beat Parma."

Gary Penrice gave Rangers a deserved lead by heading home from close range after three minutes. Devon White then had two good chances to add to that and Simon Barker saw a shot deflected wide.

But 67 seconds after the interval Merson, back from tonsilitis, jinked past three QPR players before driving home a stunning left-foot shot off the bar from 15 yards.

Wright almost added another but in the end Seaman's late save from Allen extended Arsenal's run to 19 unbeaten matches.

League Table After Match

	P	W	D	L	F	A	Pts
Man Utd.	39	25	10	4	76	37	85
Blackburn	40	25	8	7	62	34	83
Newcastle	40	22	8	10	80	39	74
Arsenal	40	18	17	5	53	24	71
Leeds	39	16	15	8	55	37	63
Wimbledon	40	17	11	12	52	49	62
Sheffield Wed	39	16	13	10	73	51	61
Liverpool	40	17	9	14	58	52	60
QPR	39	15	11	13	59	57	56
Aston Villa	40	14	12	14	43	45	54
Norwich	40	11	16	13	63	60	49
Coventry	39	12	13	14	39	43	49
Chelsea	39	12	11	16	43	47	47
West Ham	39	12	11	16	42	55	47
Man City	40	9	16	15	35	46	43
Tottenham	39	10	12	17	50	55	42
Ipswich	40	9	15	16	34	56	42
Everton	40	11	8	21	39	58	41
Southampton	39	11	6	22	42	60	39
Sheffield Utd.	39	7	17	15	37	56	38
Oldham	38	9	10	19	40	64	37
Swindon	40	4	15	21	44	94	27

April 30

ARSENAL 0

WEST HAM 2
(Half-time score: 0-0)

Arsenal: Miller, McGoldrick (Morrow), Bould, Linighan, Winterburn, Parlour, Davis, Selley, Merson (Dickov), Wright, Campbell.
Sub: Will.
West Ham: Miklosko, Breacker, Potts, Gale, Burrows, Marsh, Brown, Rush, Bishop, Allen, Morley.
Subs: Williamson, Chapman, Kelly.
Scorers: West Ham: Morley 77, Allen 88.
Referee: R Milford (Bristol)
Attendance: 33,701

League Table After Match

	P	W	D	L	F	A	Pts
Man Utd.	40	26	10	4	78	38	88
Blackburn	41	25	8	8	63	36	83
Newcastle	41	22	8	11	80	41	74
Arsenal	41	18	17	6	53	26	71
Leeds.	40	17	15	8	58	37	66
Wimbledon	41	18	11	12	54	50	65
Sheffield Wed	40	16	14	10	73	51	62
Liverpool	41	17	9	15	58	53	60
QPR	40	15	11	14	60	60	56
Aston Villa	41	14	12	15	44	49	54
Norwich	41	12	16	13	64	60	52
Coventry	40	13	13	14	41	44	52
West Ham	40	13	11	16	44	55	50
Chelsea	41	12	12	16	45	49	48
Man City	41	9	17	15	37	48	44
Tottenham	40	10	12	18	51	57	42
Southampton	40	12	6	22	46	61	42
Ipswich	41	9	15	17	35	58	42
Sheffield Utd.	40	8	17	15	39	56	41
Everton	41	11	8	22	39	61	41
Oldham	39	9	11	19	40	64	38
Swindon	41	5	15	21	47	95	30

George Graham is conservative by nature. He would rather load the gun than fire it. So there was no broadside from him about the FA's decision to deny Arsenal breathing space before their European final. But the ammunition was strategically placed.

Arsenal had just lost their first League game of 1994 – their first in 20 – with a side selected with, and distracted by, thoughts of Copenhagen.

They had asked for this match to be postponed to give them time to prepare for the Cup Winners' Cup clash final. It was not unreasonable. "I'm philosophical about things," was Graham's muted reaction. "You've got to abide by decisions and get on with it.

"It was a balancing act, giving some a rest, trying to take minds off the final and trying to win this game. I could have chanced playing others but what if injuries to Tony Adams or David Seaman had worsened?"

A roar rather than a squeak might have embarrassed the FA and Premiership, who must stand accused of narrow-minded and finicky logic. The greater success by English clubs, the greater the number allowed into European competition. The greater success, the greater the reputation of this country's game.

Skipper Adams and keeper Seaman were joined on the sidelines by Lee Dixon and Alan Smith against a West Ham team that deserved to win.

In a rare appearance, Alan Miller had saved superbly from Martin Allen, Tony Gale and Trevor Morley in the first half. But two of the three were not to be denied after the interval. Ludek Miklosko had kept out Kevin Campbell before West Ham were presented with the decisive opener.

Andy Linighan's back-pass was weak, enabling Morley to nip in, dodge the lunging Miller and score. It was just reward for the tireless front-runner. With two minutes remaining Allen, ignoring more obvious options, let fly with a cracking 25-yard drive that whistled in.

So Arsenal's alternative route to Europe next term (qualification through league position) was blocked. The only door left open was by victory in Copenhagen.

May 4

FINAL

Alan Smith, the poker-faced poacher who has led from the front for Arsenal over six seasons of outstanding achievement, brought the latest prize to the famous marble halls of Highbury.

Smith provided an object lesson in the art of centre-forward play and scored a goal of wonderful opportunism as the European Cup Winners' Cup came home from abroad.

This was a personal triumph for 32-year-old Smith from Bromsgrove, a Brummie to his size nine boots, and that dead-pan expression of his broke into a broad smile as Tony Adams collected Arsenal's first European trophy for 24 years. Smith had done much more in Copenhagen's emotionally charged Parken Stadium than score the winning goal. He had somehow exemplified the qualities that had carried Arsenal to this success.

If Ian Wright had not been suspended Smith might have been watching from the substitutes' bench, though his contribution to this exhilarating run through Europe had been enormous.

Arsenal's victory brought the total of English wins in European competitions to 24 and it ranked high among them for Arsenal had to overcome the loss not only of Wright through suspension but also of Martin Keown, John Jensen and David Hillier through injury.

During this breathless campaign George Graham has taken the map of European rule and redrawn it through outstanding tactical planning. Like a Gary Kasparov of football Graham held the cream of Europe in check until finally it was mate with Parma the victims, outwitted and outbattled.

Let nobody underestimate the quality of the Italian opposition with their nimble feet and quick minds. They had won this trophy at Wembley 12 months earlier and now they were fighting to keep it.

They are a team of such movement that opponents this season have been left feeling as if they had stepped off a fairground roller-coaster. But wherever they twisted and turned here there was a group of red shirts ready to bounce them off the ball. It was concentration of the highest order and organisation worthy of victory.

Arsenal's defensive resilience may have been a subject for derision in some quarters but ask opposition coaches what they most fear in

PARMA 0
(Half-time score: 1-0)

Arsenal: Seaman, Dixon, Winterburn, Davis, Bould, Adams, Campbell, Morrow, Smith, Merson (McGoldrick), Selley.
Subs: Linighan, Dickov, Miller.
Parma: Bucci, Benarrivo, Di Chiara, Minotti, Apolloni, Sensini, Brolin, Pin, Crippa, Zola, Asprilla.
Subs: Ballotta, Balleri, Zoratto, Melli.
Bookings: Arsenal: Adams (encroachment); Parma: Crippa (foul), Asprilla (foul).
Scorer: Arsenal: Smith 19.
Referee: Vaclav Krondl (Czech)
Attendance: 33,765

Graham's side and they will tell you it is the quality of their resistance.

Graham has said of Tony Adams that it is an honour to have worked with him and you could see why. He was not going to be fazed by the brilliance of Colombian hit-man Faustino Asprilla and Gianfranco Zola, nor be provoked by some of their more theatrical attempts to hoodwink referee Vaclav Krondl.

As usual he got on with his job of organising, of cajoling and encouraging; and, when it was all over and the battle was won, the Italian club's forwards knew which hand to shake in admiration.

So with a great leader at the back and another up front, it was a matter of others fitting in around and none deserved higher mention than goalkeeper David Seaman.

A cracked rib had necessitated a trio of pain-killing jabs and even those failed to eliminate his discomfort. Yet when it mattered most, as Arsenal protected their lead just before half-time, he faced Zola and produced an instinctive tip-over save that was a tribute to his reflexes.

But wherever the spotlight fell there were heroes. Ian Selley, a young boy from Surrey, could have been out of his depth, yet he went about his job with energy and spirit, snapping like a Jack Russell at the ankles of Parma's midfield players.

And Stephen Morrow, brought in because of the absence of John Jensen in his own country, stuck to his task of stemming Zola. His was

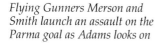
Flying Gunners Merson and Smith launch an assault on the Parma goal as Adams looks on

a discreet presence but his contribution was none the less significant.

With Jensen, Keown and Wright all absent this had seemed like sending an expedition to Everest without the sherpas. Instead Arsenal carved themselves a place as the side which restored pride to an English game which has been so damaged through Graham Taylor's era.

Arsenal did need their stroke of luck and they scored their goal only minutes after Tomas Brolin had delivered a cannonball against the Arsenal upright.

Even when Parma did get behind the Arsenal pillars of Adams and Steve Bould there was always Lee Dixon or Nigel Winterburn to tidy up. With Paul Merson muted and Kevin Campbell tightly policed it was Smith who created the problems.

The game was finely poised when Brolin hit the upright in the 14th minute. Five minutes later Arsenal made the vital break-through with a goal worthy of winning a final.

Dixon hit the ball left-footed in towards Smith and, though Lorenzo Minotti should have cut it out, he miscued an ambitious clearance and sent the ball to Smith, who took it calmly and with his own left foot, drilled it against the right-hand upright and into the net.

With Arsenal's fine defence, one sensed that might be the winner but, though the Italians lost some of their discipline, it needed Seaman's heroic save to keep the lead intact.

Adams had been cautioned for encroachment but now he was joined in the book by Massimo Crippa and Asprilla as Parma became more and more frustrated.

The Italians continued to pound Arsenal's goal in the second half when Winterburn seemed to be hit by a coin but Arsenal were not going to let go now and held on with terrific discipline to collect their deserts.

Smith said: "It was a terrific way to end the season. It has been a wonderful European campaign for the club and to come here to Copenhagen and win it and for me to score the winner was just fantastic.

"When you get one goal for Arsenal you usually feel it might be enough with the defence we have. It is also more pleasing because Italy has the reputation of being the best League in the world and they certainly have some of the best players.

"To score the winning goal has to rank alongside the best memories of my career."

George Graham said: "It was always going to be difficult for us without Wright and the other injured players. Parma are one of the best teams in Europe.

"Alan Smith was undoubtedly the man of the match. He worked

tirelessly throughout the match and held the ball up well. But there were a lot of heroes tonight.

"The Italians were superior to us on the ball and they looked fitter than us but that is down to the long slog of the English season.

"It is nice to be able to say that after we have won because they were stronger than us. But we showed a lot of character out there and there are a lot of tired players.

"From a personal viewpoint I am very happy, but happier for the

The Cup is in the safe hands of David Seaman

players because working for me is not easy. I want to win all the time and I set high standards and push them hard.

"But I don't ask them to do anything they are not capable of and the character they showed tonight was absolutely tremendous. To have beaten one of the best sides around is a terrific feeling.

"The strong part of the game was our defence and I knew that if we could get a goal there was a good chance of keeping a clean sheet. In that direction it all went according to plan."

There were no complaints from Parma manager Navio Scala who suggested : "We didn't play as well as we can but we are happy to have reached the final again. Arsenal were very strong.

"They had one shot on goal and it won them the game. But they controlled our system of play very well and I have to accept that the better side won."

May 7

For Arsenal this meeting between third- and fourth-placed clubs was little more than a fixture-completing exercise.

Where else this season has George Graham said "it doesn't matter," as he did when asked to debate the validity of Peter Beardsley's match-clinching penalty? "The last thing we needed after Wednesday in Copenhagen was another match," sighed the Highbury manager.

But for Andy Cole the match could not have come soon enough as he rounded off a remarkable season by scoring his 41st goal against his old club.

Ian Wright, subdued almost to the point of anonymity, recognised that, which is why he happily exchanged shirts with the Newcastle No 9. "He's had a fantastic season, and I am very pleased for him," said Wright.

When Newcastle went off on their end-of-season lap of honour something was missing – and Kevin Keegan knew it. It was left to Graham to provide the missing link. As he walked out of St. James' Park, Graham picked up the European Cup Winners' Cup which Arsenal had brought to show off to their Premiership friends.

It was a symbolic act and it rammed home a point to Newcastle's ambitious manager. "It's a strange thing to do a lap of honour when you haven't actually won anything," said Keegan. "Next year maybe we can put that right; that has to be our aim."

That's why Keegan is desperate to accompany Arsenal into Europe next season where, if given the opportunity, he predicts they can do as well. And that's why he's ready to make the most of a trip to the World Cup next month.

With a few million to spend, he wants to improve a Newcastle side who got closer than anyone to the two teams that slogged it out for the title.

"If I see a decent player out there who is available then we will be in," he promised. "We'll definitely be doing some business in the summer because I am not thinking about holidays at the moment, I am just thinking about next season.

"We can attract people here because we are a club at the top of a lot of players' lists."

NEWCASTLE 2

ARSENAL 0
(Half-time score: 0-0)

Newcastle: Srnicek, Venison, Beresford, Peacock, Neilson, Watson, Lee, Fox, Sellars, Beardsley, Cole.
Subs: Robinson, Jeffrey, Hooper.
Arsenal: Miller, Dixon (Linighan), Winterburn, Davis (Parlour), Adams, Bould, Morrow, Selley, McGoldrick, Wright, Smith.
Sub: Will.
Booking: Arsenal: Selley (foul).
Scorers: Newcastle: Cole 46, Beardsley (pen) 66.
Referee: R Dilkes (Mossley)
Attendance: 32,216

League Table After Match

	P	W	D	L	F	A	Pts
Man Utd.	41	27	10	4	80	38	91
Blackburn	42	25	9	8	63	35	84
Newcastle	42	23	8	11	82	41	77
Arsenal	42	18	17	7	53	28	71
Leeds	42	18	16	8	65	39	70
Wimbledon	42	18	11	13	56	53	65
Sheffield Wed	42	16	16	10	76	54	64
Liverpool	42	17	9	16	59	55	60
QPR	42	16	12	14	62	61	60
Aston Villa	42	15	12	15	46	50	57
Coventry	41	14	13	14	43	45	55
Norwich	42	12	17	13	65	61	53
West Ham	42	13	13	16	47	58	52
Chelsea	42	13	12	17	49	53	51
Tottenham	42	11	12	19	54	59	45
Man City	42	9	18	15	38	49	45
Everton	42	12	8	22	42	63	44
Southampton	42	12	7	23	49	66	43
Ipswich	42	9	16	17	35	58	43
Sheffield Utd	42	8	18	16	42	60	42
Oldham	42	9	13	20	42	68	40
Swindon	42	5	15	22	47	100	30

The
Players

David Seaman

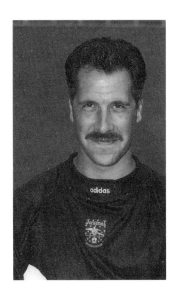

Goalkeeper; born Rotherham, September 19 1963

It was a roller-coaster season for David Seaman, who began it by missing the penalty which cost Arsenal the Charity Shield and ended by making a crucial save in the European Cup Winners' Cup final. In between he established himself as England's No1 goalkeeper in the new regime of Terry Venables.

Seaman joined Arsenal in a £1.3 million deal which was as surprising as it was costly. His arrival in May 1990 meant that George Graham was releasing John Lukic, a popular figure at Highbury who had performed so well there had been talk of an England cap.

But Seaman quickly proved his worth, securing a championship medal in 1991 as an ever present in a side which conceded 18 goals in 38 matches. And he has gone on providing the formidable last line in the country's meanest defence.

Yorkshireman Seaman began at Leeds United but did not make the first team and was sold to Peterborough for £4,000 in August 1982. He made 91 appearances there before joining Birmingham City for £100,000 as Tony Coton's replacement. He attracted interest from Manchester United, Arsenal and West Ham before moving to QPR for £225,000 in August 1986.

The 6ft 3in Seaman found towering success at Loftus Road. He won England B honours to add to his Under-21 caps and gained his first full international under Bobby Robson in the 1-1 draw against Saudi Arabia in November 1988.

His move to Highbury in 1990 helped Arsenal claim their second championship in three years. But he was dejected 12 months later when Graham Taylor left him out of the England squad for the European Championships in Sweden, preferring Chris Woods and Nigel Martyn. It turned out to be a good tournament to miss. Seaman regained his enthusiasm to help Arsenal land the Coca-Cola Cup and FA Cup double in 1993. Seaman also missed out on the 1990 World Cup when he broke a thumb in training at Calgari and was replaced by Dave Beasant. A double hernia operation last summer ruled him out of the US Cup but he has come back to make the England jersey his own.

Seaman, criticised for the Ronald Koeman free-kick which flew past him in the vital World Cup qualifier in Rotterdam last October, was sent off for the first time when he fouled West Ham's Trevor Morley a month later.

Lee Dixon

Right-back; born Manchester, March 17 1964

Lee Dixon is an attacking full-back who loves to overlap and set up many of Arsenal's attacks. He played in 32 of their Premiership matches and eight of their successful European campaign.

His father Roy was a goalkeeper with Manchester City and many of Lee's formative years were spent on the terraces at Maine Road.

But it was nearby Burnley he joined as a junior and he graduated to the senior team for a handful of games before John Bond released him to Chester. After one-and-a-half seasons there he signed for Bury and then Stoke before getting his break. He had come to George Graham's attention when Arsenal beat Stoke 3-0 in a Littlewoods Cup fourth-round tie in November 1987 and two months later the Arsenal manager signed him for £400,000.

Dixon struggled to establish himself at the end of the 1987-88 season but his surging runs from right-back and strength in the tackle were integral parts of the Gunners' team which won the title on the last day of the season at Liverpool in May 1989. Less than 12 months later he won his first England cap against Czechoslovakia.

Dixon was an ever present in Arsenal's 1991 championship side and a prolific scorer from the penalty spot before Ian Wright assumed the responsibility. He missed out on the club's Coca-Cola Cup final defeat of Sheffield Wednesday in 1993 – suspended after being sent off against Tottenham in an FA Cup semi-final – but returned to help land the FA Cup.

The low point in his international career came at the 1992 European Championships in Sweden when, after earning a surprise recall to the squad, he was injured and forced to withdraw. Despite competition from Rob Jones, Paul Parker and David Bardsley, Dixon has won 21 England caps.

Nigel Winterburn

Left-back; born Coventry, December 11 1963

Nigel Winterburn's foraging runs down the left flank became part of the folklore as little Wimbledon began their ride up the Football League. He spent four years at Plough Lane and was the club's Player of the Year in all four. His first season with the Dons under Dave Bassett ended in promotion from the Third Division and two years later Wimbledon were in the First. Winterburn's reward was his first England Under-21 cap.

Winterburn had begun at Birmingham City under Jim Smith and won England youth honours in 1980 while still an apprentice. But he failed to break into the first team, underwent an unsuccessful trial at Oxford and was given a free transfer to Wimbledon in August 1983.

His career ignited in South London. By the end of 1986-87, when Wimbledon finished sixth in the First Division Winterburn's value had soared. He was widely reported to be joining Chelsea but at the last moment George Graham stepped in to sign him for £400,000.

He began his Arsenal career as second fiddle to Kenny Sansom though he played in the 3-2 Littlewoods Cup defeat by Luton in 1988 and it was not until the start of the championship-winning 1988-89 season that Winterburn earned regular recognition.

He played in all 38 League games that season and repeated the feat in 1990-91, the only ever-present player in both campaigns. His stunning goal brought victory in a sticky Coca-Cola Cup fourth-round tie at Scarborough and he went on to winners' medals in both that and the FA Cup in 1993.

Winterburn's first full England cap came against Italy in November 1989 but he had to wait for the second until the US Cup defeat by Germany in Detroit in June 1993.

Martin Keown

Central defender and full-back; born Oxford, July 24 1966

Martin Keown became super sub for George Graham during the season, coming on 14 times in all competitions and in various positions. For the true utility defender and one of the finest man-markers in the game, second time round at Highbury has proved profitable for Martin Keown and costly for Graham. The Arsenal manager sold Keown to Aston Villa for £200,000 a month after taking the job in May 1986. Seven years later Keown was back at

Highbury but with three extra noughts to his price in a £2 million deal.

Keown first arrived at Arsenal as a 14-year-old, signing associate schoolboy forms in October 1980. He became an apprentice in June 1982 but had to wait until February 1985, while he was on loan at Brighton, to make his League debut.

He did break into the Arsenal team during the 1985-86 season before Graham's arrival heralded his departure to Aston Villa. It was not a happy move at first; Villa were immediately relegated to the Second Division. They did gain promotion the following year but after a third season with them Keown joined Everton £750,000 in August 1989. Injuries to Kevin Ratcliffe and David Watson gave him lengthy runs in the side and he established himself as first choice during the 1991-92 season before Graham brought him back.

Keown, an England youth, Under-21 and B international, made his senior international debut in a friendly against France at Wembley in February 1992. A month later he scored his one England goal in a 2-2 draw in Czechoslovakia. He also played in all three matches during England's disastrous 1992 European Championship campaign.

Tony Adams

Central defender; born Romford, October 10 1966

He has been called Donkey but Tony Adams remains a thoroughbred at the heart of Arsenal's defence...with the kick of a mule. He was the outstanding player in the European Cup Winners' Cup final against Parma, leading by example as ever.

If anyone was born to be club captain it is Adams. An Arsenal loyalist all his life, he came through the club's junior ranks, signed associate schoolboy forms in 1980 and became an apprentice in 1983. His precocious power brought him a debut against Sunderland in 1983 at the age of 17, two months before he even turned pro. He quickly collected England youth, Under-21 and B honours and became Arsenal's youngest captain at 20 when he replaced Kenny Sansom in February 1987. In the same month he made his full England debut against Spain in Madrid and went on to collect the PFA Young Player of the Year award.

Adams reached his pinnacle when he captained Arsenal to the title in 1988-89 but personal humiliation was to follow 18 months later when he was sentenced to three months in prison after crashing his car following a party. He was released after 57 days, led Arsenal to their second title in three years and was recalled to the England side after a two-year absence.

Adams had a memorable 1992-93, scoring the only goal against Spurs in the FA Cup semi-finals and lifting both the Coca-Cola and FA cups.

In a chequered England career he has missed out on both the 1990 World Cup and 1992 European Championships. Now he is firmly re-established. He has won 29 caps and scored four goals.

Steve Bould

Central defender; born Stoke, November 16 1962

Tony Adams' partner in the centre of defence and the master of the near-post flick-on, Bould earned his reward for an outstanding season when he was called into Terry Venables's England squad for the matches against Greece and Norway.

Bould began his career as a 15-year-old at Stoke and signed associate schoolboy forms in September 1978. He became an apprentice less than a year later and made his League debut at Middlesbrough in September 1981.

The 6ft 2in Bould needed a spell on loan at Torquay before breaking into the Stoke first team at the Victoria Ground in 1983-84. A year later, though, Bould was a member of the Stoke side relegated from the First Division with a record 31 defeats and only 17 points. By now Bould had been converted from right-back to the centre of defence and he continued at Stoke in the Second Division until June 1988 when he was signed by Arsenal for £390,000, five months after team-mate Lee Dixon had made the same trip.

His first season at Highbury brought a championship medal and he was ever present in their next title-winning campaign in 1990-91. Afterwards Bould was plagued by injuries and by the time he was fit again in 1993 Andy Linighan had taken his place and stolen the honours in the FA Cup final.

Bould missed the first 14 games of 1993-94 with a thigh injury but restablished himself in typically determined fashion.

John Jensen

Midfield; born Copenhagen, May 3 1965

The 5ft 8in Danish international became a cult figure at Highbury this season when fans waited in anticipation of his first goal since his arrival in the summer of 1992. His bustling, combative style was a vital influence in Arsenal's midfield until knee ligament injury ruled him out of the European final after playing in all previous ties.

Jensen caught the eye of the world and George Graham during the 1992 European Championships. Denmark began quietly against England and Sweden before beating France to move into the semi-finals against Holland. Jensen, an experienced international of eight years, was a pivotal figure, holding his injury-stricken side together as they squeezed through in a penalty shoot-out.

So to the final and tournament favourites Germany: if anything looked a football certainty it was that Germany were 90 minutes away from being crowned kings of Europe. Denmark, and Jensen, had clearly not read the script. Jensen turned the final on its head with a superb 25-yard goal and Denmark went on to create a shocking 2-0 win.

A month later Graham, clearly impressed, parted with £1.1 million to bring Jensen to Highbury. It was Jensen's third country: he had begun his career with Brondby at home in Denmark and spent a brief, unhappy spell in the German Bundesliga with SV Hamburg.

Now that goal against Germany seems a distant memory as Jensen has yet to score for Arsenal. He missed the 1993 League Cup victory but was a key figure in the FA Cup, shackling Chris Waddle.

Paul Davis

Midfield; born Dulwich, December 9 1961

Davis, the longest-serving player on the staff, and the outstanding schemer in a club sometimes accused of lacking midfield inspiration, was spotted by Arsenal as a 15-year-old and signed as an apprentice in June 1978. He made his League debut against Spurs at White Hart Lane in April 1980.

In the early days he had to battle for a midfield place against Liam Brady, John Hollins, Graham Rix and Brian Talbot. But Davis established himself in the 1981-82 season and was a Littlewoods Cup winner against Liverpool in 1987.

But the 1988-89 season, when Arsenal pipped Liverpool for the championhip in the final game of the season, was a personal mess for the talented Davis. He was suspended for nine matches and fined a record £3,000 for breaking the jaw of Southampton midfielder Glenn Cockerill. He played only 12 League games all season, missing out on a championship medal. The suspension certainly cost Davis an England career as well, he has never progressed beyond Under-21 and B honours.

But his gifted left foot was back in Arsenal's midfield in 1990-91 and he missed only one League game as Arsenal again claimed the title. He fell out with George Graham the following season and has never since commanded a regular place although he featured in both Wembley triumphs in 1993 when his experience proved invaluable.

Stephen Morrow

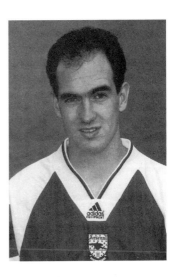

Midfield; born Belfast, July 2 1970

The Northern Irish midfield player was being carried off to hospital while his team-mates climbed the steps to the Royal Box to carry off the Coca-Cola Cup. He had won the cup with his first goal for the club...a stunning second-half strike. In the celebrations Morrow was hoisted aloft by captain Tony Adams on the pitch, toppled over his back and broke his right arm. He was carried off on a stretcher breathing through an oxygen mask and needed eight pins and a screw inserted into his arm.

Morrow was out for the rest of the season but returned to make seven appearances for the Gunners this season plus four as sub and was in the starting line-up against Parma and performed heroically.

Morrow had come to Arsenal's attention as a 14-year-old and signed at Highbury in May 1985, becoming a member of the club's FA Youth Cup-winning side of 1988.

A Northern Ireland youth and Under-21 cap, he made his full international debut before he had made a first-team appearance, coming on as a substitute against Uruguay in Belfast in May 1990. His League debut followed in January 1991 while on loan at Reading and in 1991-92 he made two League appearances for Arsenal in between turning out on loan at Watford, Reading and Barnet.

By the start of 1992-93 he had played more times for his country than for Arsenal, but an injury to Nigel Winterburn brought him back to Highbury for a spell around Christmas and he finally established himself in the side. His 50th senior appearance came in that Coca-Cola Cup final. Morrow returned to action last November.

David Hillier

Midfield; born Blackheath, December 19 1969

David Hillier, a strong tackler, began with Arsenal as an associate schoolboy in January 1984 and became a trainee two years later. He was a key figure in the club's FA Youth Cup-winning run in 1988.

His first-team chance came in a Rumbelows Cup tie at Chester in September 1990 because Michael Thomas was injured and Siggi Jonsson was playing for Iceland. His League debut followed quickly at Leeds and he went on to make another 15 appearances that season, earning a championship medal. He was rewarded with an England Under-21 cap.

Hillier's strong tackling established him further the following season – especially with Paul Davis out of favour – and he was a regular at the heart of the midfield in 1992-93.

He was instrumental in Arsenal's double-pronged assault on Wembley but 12 days after the Coca-Cola Cup final he was injured in a 1-0 defeat at Middlesbrough and did not play again that season.

Hillier, 5ft 10in, forced his way back into the team with difficulty. He made seven appearances, plus four as sub, but his two goals in more than 100 Arsenal games is a record that stands improvement.

Ray Parlour

Midfield; born Romford, March 7 1973

Nicknamed Shirley Temple by his team-mates because of his flowing, curly locks, Ray Parlour is a possible star for the future. He established himself in the first team with 24 starts and three appearances as sub, scoring twice.

Parlour joined Arsenal as a trainee in July 1989 having been on associate schoolboy forms for the previous 18 months. He turned professional in March 1991 and made a surprise breakthrough in the 1991-92 season, his League debut coming at Liverpool in January 1992 when he was just 18. That summer he was awarded a starting place with England Under-21 in the annual Toulon tournament.

In 1993 Parlour played an important role in the 2-1 Coca-Cola Cup victory over Sheffield Wednesday. His FA Cup experience a few weeks later, though, was a mixed one. Parlour played in the forgettable 1-1 draw and was then dropped for the replay to make way for Alan Smith.

It was a disappointing end to a memorable season and 1993-94 started the same way. He struggled to find form and spent the first four months on the edge of the first team.

Paul Merson

Midfield; born Harlesden, March 20 1968

George Graham's inconsistent use of Paul Merson, an eye-catching wing man or striker, brought much head-shaking among the Highbury faithful. But he finished the season on a high note with a storming performance for England B in their 4-2 victory over Northern Ireland on May 10, scoring one goal and making another.

The England international – 13 caps so far – had become a favourite with his looping runs and storming goals. But the Arsenal manager seemed unconvinced and there were rumours of transfer movement. But Merson looks too valuable for Arsenal to sell. He scored 12 goals in his 38 appearances in all competitions.

Merson came through the junior ranks at Arsenal and made his League debut against Manchester City in November 1986. He had a spell on loan at Brentford in 1986-87 before starting to establish himself with the Gunners the following season. By 1988-89 he was a regular and scored 10 League goals, missing only one game, as Arsenal nicked the title off Liverpool. Merson was named PFA Young Player of the Year.

Playing as a striker, he missed only two games in the 1990-91 season as Arsenal won the championship again. This time he grabbed 13 goals alongside the prolific Alan Smith.

Merson, an England youth, Under-21 and B international, was rewarded for another excellent season with his first full cap against Germany at Wembley in September 1991, coming on for John Salako. He played in two of England's three European Championship matches in Sweden in 1992 and by now was operating almost exclusively as a winger for both club and country.

Merson had a big part to play in both cup runs in 1992-93. In the Coca-Cola final he scored a 25-yard equaliser and performed so outstandingly overall he won the Alan Hardaker Trophy as man of the match. In the FA Cup his stunning equaliser at home to Leeds in the fourth round kept Arsenal on course for Wembley, where he starred again in the final.

Ian Wright

Striker; born Woolwich, November 3 1963

The abiding memory of Ian Wright was of his tears when his semi-final booking at Highbury ruled him out of the final of the European Cup Winners' Cup. But in truth it was a glorious season of triumph for Wright, who scored 34 goals in all competitions, including 23 in the League.

George Graham realised what a gem he had and rewarded Wright for his outstanding ability with a new four-year contract worth £1 million which will keep him at Highbury until he is 33.

Wright, who had feared he might be ignored by new England coach Terry Venables, also found himself called into the squad for the friendly internationals against Greece and Norway in May and hopeful of adding to his 16 caps and six international goals.

Wright's habit of scoring spectacular goals began at non-League Greenwich Borough before he joined Crystal Palace in 1985 and forged a devastating partnership with Mark Bright. He made his Palace debut against Huddersfield in August 1985 in the Second Division and after a couple of relatively quiet seasons exploded into the limelight with 20 League goals in 1987-88 and 24 in 1988-89 as Palace moved into the First Division via the play-offs.

His first season in the top flight was a disaster as he twice broke a leg. But he returned in time for the Cup final against Manchester United and scored twice in a 3-3 draw before United won the replay.

After scoring five goals in eight games at the start of the 1991-92 season he was sold to Arsenal for £2.5 million in September 1991. He scored for the Gunners on his debut against Leicester in the Rumbelows Cup and finished the season as First Division top scorer with 29 goals, 24 of them for Arsenal.

The following season he collected a Coca-Cola Cup winners' medal and then scored in both games during the FA Cup final success over Sheffield Wednesday. Fiery at times, Wright was banned for three matches after punching Spurs player David Howells.

Wright's first England cap came against Cameroon in February 1991, but his international record for such a prolific striker is a poor one. In his first 15 internationals he scored once...before landing four in the 7-1 demolition of San Marino.

Kevin Campbell

Striker; born Lambeth, February 4 1970

This was the season when Kevin Campbell really arrived on the big scene. Inconsistent at times, he still managed to finish with 19 goals from 41 starts in all competitions, plus another 13 appearances as substitute.

The muscular 6ft striker used his blazing speed to unsettle even the best defences although his occasional haste with the final shot wrecked some promising moves.

Campbell became an associate schoolboy at Arsenal in 1985, picking the Gunners ahead of Millwall, Charlton and Chelsea. He had a phenomenal season for the youths and reserves during 1987-88, scoring 59 goals, including a hat-trick in the 6-1 FA Youth Cup success over Doncaster. He was rewarded with his League debut at Everton in the final game of the season.

Even so, he failed to dislodge Smith and Wright as Arsenal's main strike force the following season and was sent to Leyton Orient on loan where he scored nine goals in 16 games. He also had a stint at Leicester.

Campbell, an England Under-21 and B international, scored four times as Arsenal reached the Coca-Cola Cup final in 1993 and played in both Wembley successes against Sheffield Wednesday.

Alan Smith

Striker; born Bromsgrove, November 21 1962

Alan Smith will never score a more important or perfectly struck goal than the one which took the European Cup Winners' Cup to Highbury. His left-foot shot in Copenhagen stunned Parma and could have persuaded George Graham to keep Smith at Highbury despite his 31 years and the emergence of Kevin Campbell.

Before signing as a professional with Leicester, Smith played for non-League Alvechurch and, while there, earned semi-professional England honours. He scored 13 League goals in his first season with Leicester, helping them finish third in the Second Division and win promotion into the top flight.

For three seasons he forged a wonderful partnership with Gary Lineker before Lineker left for Everton. In Smith's final season with the club they were relegated and he signed for Arsenal for £850,000 in March 1987 as Leicester's battle against the drop became forlorn.

He was an instant hit with Arsenal and topped their scoring charts in four of his first five seasons. The first season, in fact, ended with a Littlewoods Cup final appearance at Wembley where he scored in a 3-2 defeat by Luton. The following season was his best with 23 goals from 36 League games, the most important being the first in the 2-0 defeat of Liverpool which clinched the championship.

He was top scorer again when Arsenal claimed the title in 1991 but then the goals dried up and he has battled with Kevin Campbell for the position alongside Wright. He was an unused sub in the Coca-Cola Cup triumph against Sheffield Wednesday after scoring twice in the 3-1 semi-final first leg at Crystal Palace. But he played in the FA Cup success, also against Wednesday, when he was booked for the first time in his career.

Smith gained his first full England cap against Saudi Arabia in November 1988. The last of his 13 caps came when he replaced Lineker in the 2-1 defeat by Sweden in the 1992 European Championships.

Anders Limpar
Born Solna, September 24 1965

The Swedish international delighted Highbury fans with his skill but frustrated George Graham with his inconsistency. He was signed for £1 million from Italian club Cremonese in August 1990 and won a championship medal in 1991, scoring a hat-trick against Coventry in the final match of the season. But he faded from the scene and was sold to Everton for £1.4 million in March.

Ian Selley
Born Chertsey, June 14 1974

Tough-tackling midfielder who is one of George Graham's real hopes for the future. He made 16 League appearances for the Gunners this season plus two as sub. He signed associate schoolboy forms in October 1988 and turned pro during the 1992 close season.

Andy Linighan
Born Hartlepool, June 18 1962

A strong central defender who acts as cover for Adams and Bould. He made 20 League appearances this season. Andy began his career at Hartlepool and joined Leeds for £200,000 in May 1984. He moved to Oldham for £65,000 in 1986, was signed by Norwich as replacement for Steve Bruce for £350,000 in 1988 and moved to Arsenal for £1.2 million in July 1990. An England B international, he scored the extra-time winner to beat Sheffield Wednesday in the FA Cup final replay.

Alan Miller
Born Epping, March 29 1970

Seaman's understudy whose chances have been limited. He joined Highbury as a schoolboy in 1984 and made his League debut while on loan to Plymouth in November 1988. He has also played for Birmingham and West Brom on loan. An England youth and Under-21 international, Miller made his Arsenal debut in November 1992 against Leeds.

Eddie McGoldrick
Born Islington, April 30 1965

McGoldrick signed for Arsenal for £1 million in June 1993 from Crystal Palace but has been criticised by sections of the Highbury fans who were looking for George Graham to buy a more obvious star. McGoldrick, who plays midfield or wide full-back has made 23 League appearances without truly establishing himself and was expected to return to Crystal Palace during the close season. The Republic of Ireland international has not scored a League goal for Arsenal but was on target during the 7-0 defeat of Standard Liege in the European Cup Winner's Cup second round.

George Graham

Manager, born Glasgow, November 30 1944.

Since he left Millwall for Arsenal eight years ago, George Graham has re-established the Gunners as one of the foremost teams in the country with a sustained period of success not seen at Highbury since the days of Herbert Chapman.

Yet, despite his triumph with two League championships, the League Cup, FA Cup and now the European Cup Winners' Cup, Graham is a man who is able to find time for hobbies. He has an aficionado's collection of Arsenal memorabilia, a connoisseur's selection of malt whiskies and he loves gardening.

"Hobbies keep you sane," he says. "The pressures are always there: games to play, games to see, people to talk to, angles to work out. All day and every day. Unless you're careful there's nothing else."

Graham has proved more adept than most at handling that pressure. He remains a fierce disciplinarian, ruling the club with a firm hand that stems from his Glaswegian background. His father died on Christmas Day when George was three years old and the tough attitudes he gathered in the following years have fashioned his current philosophy.

Not that one would have realised that backbone of steel from his playing days. A cultured Scottish international midfield player who was crucial in the Arsenal Double season of 1971, Graham was nicknamed "Stroller" because of his nonchalant image on the field. But as soon as he was handed the chance of management at Millwall he displayed an unrelenting search for success.

Graham's career began as an apprentice at Aston Villa in December 1961 and progressed through transfers to Chelsea, Arsenal, Manchester United, Portsmouth and Crystal Palace. His most successful and productive spell was undoubtedly at Arsenal where he made 219 appearances between 1966 and 1972 and scored 60 goals.

His ruthless brand of management has been in evidence since he joined Arsenal in 1986. Terrace adulation failed to preserve a Highbury future for Kenny Sansom and Charlie Nicholas and latter-day stars such as Michael Thomas and David Rocastle were shipped out when they least expected it.

"Winning is an obsession," says Graham, who has been promised a job for life at Highbury. "It is also a magnificent obsession. I have loved this job every moment since I got it."

Great Players
of the Past

Eddie Hapgood

They called Eddie Hapgood the Ambassador of Football because he was captain both of the great Arsenal team of the Thirties and of England.

Arsenal were then rated unofficial club champions of the world and played exhibitions throughout Europe; England considered themselves by right to be pre-eminent even though they had declined to take part in the embryonic World Cup.

Hapgood, usually a left-back although he could play in other defensive positions, was admired for the elegance of his play and his ball skills. Such was his ability he was even accused of showing off by others less gifted.

He was always football mad and as a boy was called before the local magistrates in his home town of Bristol and warned about his "passion for kicking a ball which could land you in trouble". He is believed to have damaged a flower bed or two and also to have taken time off school.

When he was old enough Bristol Rovers offered him a contract which included the summer employment of driving a coal cart. He declined and instead joined non-League Kettering before moving to Arsenal where he gained five Championship and two FA Cup winners' medals.

He made his debut for England in 1933 at the age of 22 and collected a then record 30 caps in an international career shortened by the Second World War. He was captain of England during the notorious 1938 match with Germany in Berlin's Olympic Stadium when, under diplomatic pressure, it was agreed the England team would give the Nazi salute during the playing of Deutschland über Alles.

The Germans had also agreed to stand for the British National Anthem but the resultant pictures of Hapgood and his players with their arms outstretched provoked fury in an England teetering on the edge of war with Germany. Hapgood had argued strenuously against the action. In the end he and his England team had the finest riposte, winning 6-3.

Hapgood made 487 appearances for Arsenal in all matches before retiring in 1940.

Cliff Bastin

One of the most dashing wingers of all time, he was nicknamed "Boy" Bastin because he had won almost every honour in the game by his 21st birthday.

Born in Devon he was one of the key figures in Herbert Chapman's great Thirties team, terrorising defences with his speed and control. He was paid the ultimate compliment by the great Austrian manager Hugo Meisl. After his Wunderteam had lost to Italy in the semi-finals of the 1934 World Cup, Meisl was asked what his team had lacked to win the competition. He answered: Cliff Bastin.

Bastin had begin his career at his local club Exeter City and was in their League team at the age of 15, a year after being capped by England at schoolboy level. Chapman signed him in May 1929 for £2,000 and Bastin quickly established himself in the Gunners' first team. He was soon picking up honours as well: an FA Cup winners' medal in 1930 against Huddersfield, a League Championship medal the following season as Arsenal won the title for the first time, and his first full international cap against Wales at Liverpool in November 1931. Honours came regularly throughout Bastin's career and he finished with five Championship medals, two FA Cup winners' medals and one runners-up medal, plus three FA Charity Shield trophies. He gained 21 international caps between 1931 and 1938, scoring 12 goals, and appeared four times for the Football League, scoring four goals.

Although Bastin performed equally well at inside-forward and later at wing-half, his goalscoring feats from his main position as a winger were remarkable and his 33 goals in 42 matches from the wing in 1932-33 remains a Football League record.

If the war had not interrupted his career, who knows what he might have achieved? A troublesome knee and deafness affected him in his later playing years and he retired in 1947. After a short spell as a journalist and a restaurant owner, he returned to Exeter and became a publican.

Alex James

He was nicknamed Wee Alex but James was a giant for the Arsenal of the Thirties, their playmaker and inspiration at inside-forward. He was the archetype tanner ball-player from Scotland with twinkling feet and destructive passing.

Born in Mossend, Lanarkshire in 1901, James began his career with Raith Rovers in 1922 but went south to join Preston North End three years later. Herbert Chapman saw him as the key figure, midfield linkman and schemer, in his new formation and paid £8,750 to sign him in 1929. James played a crucial role in Arsenal's FA Cup victory of 1930 and went on to win four Championship medals with the club.

Astonishingly he won only eight Scottish caps - his supporters blamed an insular attitude north of the border - but he was a vital member of the Wembley Wizards who thrashed England 5-1 at Wembley in 1928. "His tongue went like a gramophone but so did his feet," said his captain that day, Hugh Taylor.

James, of the outlandishly long shorts, was certainly an outspoken character and had frequent disagreements with Chapman who indulged his genius.

James, who owned a sweetshop round the corner from Highbury, retired from playing in 1937 to become a journalist and coach until his early death at the age of 52 from cancer.

Frank McLintock

Frank will be immortalised as the inspirational captain who led the Gunners to their League and FA Cup Double in 1971. He had already played in two losing FA Cup finals with Leicester, in 1961 and 1963, before he joined Arsenal in 1964 and formed an impressive partnership at centre-back with one of Highbury's more unsung heroes Peter Simpson.

McLintock made up for a relative lack of height and speed by being a great reader of the game in the Bobby Moore mould. But he was also surprisingly agile and his heading ability made him a great asset not only in defence but also from set-pieces in attack.

He epitomised the indomitable spirit of the 1971 team which was neither massively skilful nor hugely entertaining but utterly determined and professional, well disciplined and highly organised. He proved himself a great captain in that era and was judged Footballer of the Year in 1971. He gained nine caps for Scotland between 1963-1971, a figure many felt should have been doubled.

In 1973 he moved to QPR where he formed another fine partnership with David Webb and helped them to their highest League position – second in the First Division in 1976, only one point behind Liverpool. Frank, who began his career with Shawfield Juniors in his home town of Glasgow, worked in management and coaching at Leicester, Brentford and Millwall after retiring and helped Millwall win the Second Division championship in 1988. More recently he has been a players' agent and analyst on radio and TV.

Charlie George

Charlie was the local boy made good. He was from Islington, long haired and faintly rebellious, yet destined to be canonised by Gunners' fans for the goal he scored in the 1971 Cup final which clinched the Double.

The abiding image of that sensational season for Arsenal is of George prostrate on the Wembley pitch, arms outstretched, after hitting a superb shot from outside the box that gave Arsenal an extra-time 2-1 victory over Liverpool.

George was an attacking midfield player behind the formidable partnership of John Radford and Ray Kennedy. He possessed good control, vision and the ability to hit the killer long pass. Those touches of magic plus his occasional explosive goal made him a true crowd pleaser during his five years at Highbury.

Arsenal sold him to Derby in 1975 where he was played as a front striker and scored 34 goals in 100 League games during his three-year spell there. It was while at the Baseball Ground that he won his only England cap, playing in the 1-1 draw against Eire at Wembley in September 1976 until manager Don Revie substituted him with Gordon Hill.

Lawrie McMenemy paid Derby £400,000 to take George to Southampton in 1978. But a knee injury that proved to be worse than suspected limited him to 22 games before he went on loan to Nottingham Forest. He later trained with Chelsea in an attempt to revive his colourful career but was forced to retire.

George Armstrong

Along with Frank McLintock and goalkeeper Bob Wilson, George Armstrong was the only Arsenal player to appear in all 42 League matches during the Double season of 1970-71.

His hard work and determined runs down the flank made an enormous contribution to the 34 goals scored by twin strikers John Radford and Ray Kennedy that season. Armstrong added seven himself but it was his prodigious energy and willingness to shoulder responsibility which endeared him to the crowd.

Born in Hebburn in the North-East, he was almost inevitably called Geordie after joining Arsenal in 1961. He was a players' player and Don Howe, the Arsenal coach in 1971, said: "He was a terrific grafter with enormous stamina. He used to win the cross-country races regularly at the club and it was his running and covering that allowed George Graham to get forward and score so many goals. He was also a wonderful striker of the ball, so good in fact that he took corners from both sides of the field."

An England Under-23 international, Armstrong could play on either wing, although he favoured the left, and if Arsenal were facing a particularly dangerous opponent, Armstrong would switch to cover the full-back. When he left to join Leicester in 1976, Arsenal tried a number of wingers like Peter Marinello and Graham Rix without finding that same combination of defensive strength and attacking ability.

He played 490 games plus ten as sub in 16 seasons with Arsenal, scoring 53 goals himself and memorably supplying the left-wing cross that Kennedy headed into the Tottenham net to win the League title in 1971. He was in the Cup final team five days later and appeared in the losing final against Leeds the following year.

After one season with Leicester he finished his career with Stockport County. He has returned to Highbury as youth team coach.

Joe Mercer

Mercer was in his thirties when the Second World War ended and he was able to revive a football career that had started with such promise at Everton. He joined Arsenal, switched from attacking wing-half to defensive wing-half and captained the side which won the League title in 1948 and 1953 as well as the FA Cup in 1950 when he was voted Footballer of the Year.

Mercer's father had been captain of Nottingham Forest before the First World War and had been taken prisoner and died at the age of 37. Joe left school at 14 and did manual jobs before signing for Everton at 15, a club bursting with international footballers.

Mercer became a pro at 17 and won a Championship medal with Everton in 1939 having made his debut for England the year earlier. By the time the Second World War took him away he had won five caps as an attacking wing-half and went on to play for England 26 times more during and immediately after the war before he damaged a cartilage.

Then Tom Whittaker took an apparent gamble and paid £7,000 to bring Mercer to Arsenal. It proved to be a master-stroke. Mercer adapted his game. "I couldn't attack any more," he said. "I had to learn to tuck in behind the centre-half." The Gunners, second from the bottom of the First Division when he arrived, comfortably avoided relegation. They won the title the following season, 1947-48, and again in 1952-53. Mercer's wily leadership also helped them carry off the FA Cup in 1950.

His astonishing career did not end until the age of 38 when he broke a leg in a collision with a team-mate soon after Arsenal's second title win. He had played 293 games for the Gunners.

He joined Sheffield United as manager in 1955 and moved to Aston Villa in 1958, leading them to victory in the League Cup before retiring though ill health in 1964. A year later, though, he was back as manager of Manchester City and, together with coach Malcolm Allison, steered the club to its greatest era, winning the League Championship in 1968, the FA Cup in 1969 and the double of League Cup and European Cup Winners' Cup in 1970. He stood in as temporary replacement as manager of England after the sacking of Sir Alf Ramsey in 1974.

Ted Drake

Nearly 70,000 people were at Highbury on December 14, 1935, to watch the greatest solo blitz by a First Division goalscorer. Ted Drake, of the baggy shorts and mighty boots, hit seven goals for Arsenal against Aston Villa.

A hat-trick in the first half preceded four more in the second but, typically, Drake remembered only his other shot of the match. "It hit the bar," he says. "I groaned and referee Jim Wiltshire asked me, 'How many more do you want'?"

That was typical of Drake, one of the game's greatest centre-forwards who began life as a fitter for the Southampton Gas Company. He was earning 75p a week when Southampton FC spotted him playing local amateur soccer with Winchester City and offered him £3 a week plus £1 for each first-team appearance.

He was 21 when Arsenal approached him and he decided he had to try his hand in the highest League. His strong, direct approach was an instant success at the Gunners and he was capped by his country in an international career cut short by the War.

Drake was renowned for his belligerence as a barnstorming striker. He survived three damaged cartilages, fractured wrists and almost weekly repairs to temple and eyebrows.

But during a wartime match at Reading in 1945 he slipped a disc in his back and his playing days were over. He attended a two-year management course at Highbury designed to help him into a new career and was appointed manager of Reading in 1947, a job he held until his appointment as manager of Chelsea in 1952.

At Stamford Bridge he introduced a youth policy which was second only to Matt Busby's at Manchester United. His players were nicknamed Drake's Ducklings. He was fired by Chelsea in 1961 to make way for Tommy Docherty and later joined Vic Buckingham at Barcelona as coach before moving to Fulham as a scout.

Jack Kelsey

In 12 seasons at Arsenal Jack Kelsey won only one major medal but, in terms of popularity and respect, the Welsh goalkeeper was an outstanding champion. Born of a Cockney father and a Welsh mother, Kelsey was raised in Llansamlet, South Wales. Jack's dad was a smelter-furnaceman who organised a little football club called Winch Wen. By the age of five Jack was the club mascot.

His first goalkeeping hero was not Fred Stansbridge of nearby Swansea but Billo Staddon of Winch Wen FC. Kelsey would stand behind his goal and watch in awe.

When he left school at 14 Jack went into the local tin-plate works and the heavy lifting helped his physique. He played for Winch Wen Juniors, eventually replacing Staddon in the senior side. In one match Jack saved two penalties and at the end Les Morris, a former Arsenal player who had taken one of the spot kicks, offered him a trial at Highbury.

He passed with flying colours and was signed by Tom Whittaker.

In 1950-51 Kelsey broke into the first team when Swindin was injured...and Arsenal lost 5-2 to Charlton, the first time in 25 years they had conceded five goals at Highbury. Kelsey went on to make another 326 appearances for Arsenal, collecting a Championship medal in 1953. He won 41 caps for Wales.

While playing for his country Kelsey won only 10 times. Wales drew 13 and lost 18 but in 1958 he received the ultimate accolade during the World Cup finals in Sweden. In the quarter-final Kelsey dived to save the shot of a 17-year-old Brazilian called Pele and watched in horror as the ball spun off the boot of a defender and into the net. "That was my luckiest goal," Pele wrote later. "Kelsey was a wonderful goalkeeper."

Jack's playing career was brought to a premature end playing against Brazil in Sao Paulo four years later. Kelsey dived at the feet of Vava and the forward's knee caught him in the back. He tried to throw the ball out but his back locked. X-rays at home showed a congenital deformity of the spine. At the age of 33 Jack was forced to retire...and take his friendly personality to the Gunners' shop.

Liam Brady

In an era which relied more and more on power, strength and defensive organisation, Liam Brady offered a touch of creative class. The best player the Republic of Ireland has produced, Brady was born in Dublin in 1956 and, encouraged by his great-uncle Frank – who captained the Republic of Ireland during the Fifties – and older brothers Ray and Pat, both capped at senior level by Eire, he showed at an early age he had a talent for the game, winning a host of medals with St Kevin's the best junior side in Dublin.

He was spotted by Arsenal at the age of 13 and signed for them after a trial. Manchester United and Coventry were also after him.

From then until his £600,000 transfer to Italian giants Juventus in 1980, "Chippy" Brady and his cultured left foot provided the silky skills behind the steel which helped Arsenal reach three consecutive FA Cup finals between 1978 and 1980 – beating Manchester United in 1979 – and the European Cup Winners' Cup final.

He was capped at 18 by Johnny Giles and went on to break Giles's long-standing record of 59 caps during a glorious international career stretching over 16 years. Under the management of Jack Charlton, Brady captained the Republic to the finals of the European Nations Championships in West Germany in June 1988. He had joined West Ham by this time and a serious knee injury incurred in a League match against Derby four months earlier forced him to miss out.

The Republic also qualified for the World Cup in 1990 but Brady had already decided to retire at the end of that domestic season. Don Howe, who was associated with Arsenal for 22 years and worked with Brady throughout his career there, says: "Brady was the greatest talent Arsenal or world football saw during that time." Brady tried his hand at management with Celtic before moving to Brighton.

The Future

For once George Graham was prepared to forget about his relentless pursuit of silverware. As the plane swept home from Copenhagen to the clink of champagne bottles and the glint of the European Cup Winners' Cup, the Arsenal manager insisted he was thrusting his mind into neutral for the next couple of days.

"I'm not even going to consider the future for at least 48 hours," he said. "You have to celebrate your triumphs in this game. Goodness knows, they're hard enough to achieve. Let's all relax and recharge ourselves. Then we'll consider the challenges that await us."

Those include the defence of the cup Arsenal wrested off Parma and, of course, a more sustained challenge on the citadel of Old Trafford.

Graham knows he must strengthen his squad for those tasks. Wheeling and dealing in players is all part of the Graham technique even if he manages to keep his transfer moves far more low key than the likes of Kenny Dalglish and Alex Ferguson.

His strict Scottish upbringing may make Graham less likely to part with Arsenal's hard-earned cash, yet he admits he would be tempted to enter the chase for Norwich's exciting striker Chris Sutton, rated at £4 million, and QPR's international goalscorer Les Ferdinand.

Dalglish and Blackburn Rovers, backed by Jack Walker's millions, had reportedly put aside £4.75 million to bid for Ferdinand during the close season and QPR chairman Richard Thompson was not expected to turn down such a massive offer. But Graham, who knows the value of paying good money for a striker after his bold move for Ian Wright, is a definite Ferdinand fan. He could be ready to offer cash and a player exchange to QPR.

That could mean farewell to Highbury for Alan Smith, European matchwinner in Copenhagen, who had been linked with a move to Japan and Grampus Eight, the club his old Leicester team-mate Gary Lineker joined. Smith, though, was keen to remain at Arsenal even if it meant playing in the reserves.

One player who seemed certain to be signed by Graham was Benfica's Swedish midfielder Stefan Schwarz, rated at 1.5 million. The player's agent Vincenzo Moravito had met with Graham reportedly to finalise the deal.

Arsenal were keen to sign Schwarz before the summer's World Cup, knowing that an impressive performance by him in America would attract other interest and increase his value.

As ever Graham was keeping his cards close to his chest. He delighted in his signing of Wright for £2.5 million in September 1991 while he (Graham) was playing in the Football Writers' Golf Day. "There's a surprise for you," he said as the office phones started ringing to drag journalists away from the bar and locker room.

He knows his duty, though, to the fans who turned out in their hundreds of thousands to welcome back the team as they travelled in an open-top bus through the streets of Highbury and Islington. "It's wonderful to see so many," he said. "It's their day as much as ours. We're just pleased we have a trophy to show them because their support in Copenhagen was magnificent.

"It would be nice to be doing the same thing next year with another trophy or two to put in the cabinet. That has to be our goal: at least one trophy a season. That's the yardstick we have to use to judge the players we bring to Highbury. I'm not looking for a crowd pleaser. I want good players who can perform week in and week out at the highest level. They have to realise that one good game in three is not enough. They must perform three times a week for 10 months of the year.

"You see certain teams who lift their game when they play the likes of us or United and then have a dodgy result the following week. We can't afford to do that."

The way ahead, Graham suggested, might be for Arsenal to look for a little more flair. "The final League places were a true reflection of ability," he said. "We know our strengths and weaknesses. We just don't want to be beaten but sometimes I think we could go forward and entertain a bit more. I think that will come."

International call-ups for Steve Bould, Paul Merson and Wright, in addition to Tony Adams, as Terry Venables continued to fashion his new England side, kept spirits high. And Graham himself was given a huge – and sincere – vote of confidence from vice chairman David Dein. "He has proved to be ambitious and then more ambitious," he said. "Long may it continue. He has done a magnificent job at Highbury and surrounded himself with excellent people both on and off the pitch."

Acknowledgements

Fred Ollier and his book *Arsenal: A Complete Record* for the
Great Players of the Past chapter.

Frances Jennings and John Cross
for helping to compile statistics.

Jeremy Alexander for all his help and hard work.

Clive and Sandra Gordon and all at SLG for their
tremendous help and support.

Picture copyright all *Daily Express* except:
page 123: Kappa Sports Pictures.
pages 136 (Tony Adams) and 143 (Alan Smith):
Universal Pictorial.
Colour Section page 22 (top and bottom): PA News.